ART NOW

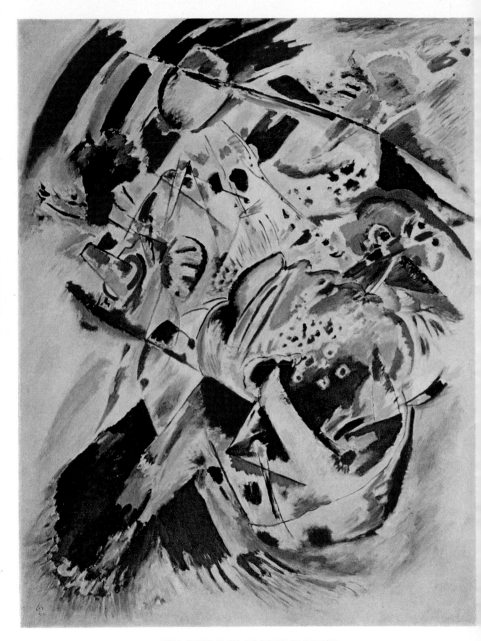

WASSILLY KANDINSKY
Winter

ART NOW

an introduction to the
theory of modern painting and sculpture
by
HERBERT READ

FABER AND FABER LIMITED
24 Russell Square
London

*First published in October mcmxxxiii
by Faber & Faber Ltd
24 Russell Square London WC1
Revised editions: mcmxxxvi & mcmxlviii
Revised & enlarged edition: mcmlx
Printed in Great Britain
by R. MacLehose & Co Limited
Glasgow*

PREFACE TO THE
REVISED EDITION OF 1960

This book was first published in 1933; revised editions were published in 1936 and 1948, but all this time and until the present day modern art has continued its course, and even in the last fifteen years has shown surprising new developments.

The book was originally planned as a theoretical exposition of the principles underlying the modern movement, but it always suffered the dichotomy represented by the main-title and the sub-title: the text aimed to be definitive, but the illustrations were topical, and as successive editions appeared, had to be revised and increased to do justice to the changing state of painting and sculpture. But step by step the text also had to be changed, the necessary adjustments being made by additional prefaces and an epilogue.

What I have done in this new, and I hope final edition of the book is to return to my original intention and make the text a self-sufficient exposition of principles. I trace the origins and development of the modern movement, not in the historical events nor even in the technical inventions of the artists, but in the changes of mental climate that accompanied these inventions and events. I do not assume that the mental climate was the determining cause of the changing forms of art—those who have read my *Icon and Idea* will realize that my general belief is quite the contrary. But perception and intellection, technical invention and philosophical generalization, have a dialectical relationship and together they weave the fabric of art history. In the text of this book I am unravelling one essential thread of that process: the illustrations are there to represent the other thread.

[7]

I will reproduce the substance of two paragraphs from the Preface to the first edition of 1933, because though they were written in a period of acute political stress, the confusion they deal with still exists—the tendency to identify the modern movement in art with whatever the reactionary mind considers socially or politically undesirable—communism or fascism. The savage treatment which modern art and artists have received in Russia and Germany should have dispelled the last traces of this false identification, but we still find it repeated.[1] Admittedly modern art assumes the inevitability of a disintegration of the cultural values of the immediate past—so does the original art of every fertile age. But the revolutionary artist is not for that reason to be identified with the revolutionary politician. He works on another plane where his activities are determined by that wider destiny which governs all the activities of the human spirit. If anything, the more 'modern' he is in spirit, the more disinterested and detached he becomes. In short, the good artist has very rarely a practical interest in anything but his art.

So much is a matter of present fact; but in this book I hope I have shown further that even in its origins and development the modern movement in art has nothing whatsoever to do with sentiments external to its nature. We may find an historical connection between that movement and the general course of culture and civilisation since the Renaissance; but not only modern art, but modern ideas of every sort, including certainly the ideas underlying fascism and nationalism, are the outcome of the same anonymous tradition. Modern art is inevitably modern; but its modernity is expressed in terms that are strictly artistic, and these are the result

---

[1] For example, by Sir Charles Snow in the Rede Lecture of 1959: 'It is no use denying the facts, which are broadly true. The honest answer was that there is, in fact, a connection, which literary persons are culpably slow to see, between some kinds of early twentieth-century art and the most imbecile expressions of anti-social feeling.' *The Two Cultures and the Scientific Revolution*, 1959, pp. 7–8.

of developments within the technique and science of art. The great artists who have most determined the course of modern art—Constable, Turner, Cézanne, Matisse, Picasso, Kandinsky, Klee—have been and are singularly devoid of ideological motivation. They have lived in their vision and their paint, and have followed the inevitable course dictated by their sensibility.[1]

That their reliance on their sensibility may have had revolutionary consequences is perhaps to be admitted; but that too is an inevitable tendency of the modern spirit. The more mechanical the world becomes (not only the visible world, but the actual process of living) the less spiritual satisfaction there is to be found in the appearances of this world. The inner world of the imagination becomes more and more significant, as if to compensate for the poverty and the drabness of every-day life. This process of compensation has taken place in other historical periods, and art as strange and incomprehensible as any to be seen to-day may be found in the past. But not in the immediate past. The prejudice against modern art is, I am convinced, the result of a confined vision or a narrow range of sensibility. People forget that the artist (if he deserves that name) has the acutest sense of us all; and he can only be true to himself and to his function if he expresses that acuteness to the final edge. We are without courage, without freedom, without passion and joy, if we refuse to follow where he leads.

August 1959   H.R.

[1] Picasso, I know, may be quoted as an exception. But one major painting ('Guernica') and a formal but wholly ambiguous adhesion to the Communist Party, do not exempt him from this generalisation.

CONTENTS

CONTENTS

III. EXPRESSIONISM

CONTENTS

LIST OF ILLUSTRATIONS

COLOUR PLATES

MONOCHROME PLATES
at the end of the book

[15]

Chapter I

BACKGROUND
FROM REYNOLDS TO BERGSON:

REVOLUTION IN THE
THEORETICAL CONCEPTION OF ART

I want, in this first chapter, to trace a gradual change in the general philosophy of art that has prepared the way for the practice of modern art. We must go back a long way—in fact, to the beginnings of the empirical method in criticism. We shall then find a growing awareness of the diversity of art and, as more and more manifestations of the artist's will come under the review of philosophers, the old *a priori* method becomes inadequate, and finally fails: a new science is born, the science of art. It is a science which admits evidence from many fields hitherto not associated with the philosophy of beauty—evidence from history and anthropology, from religion and psychology, from morphology and philology—from every field that deals with the spirit of man and the modes of its expression. The difference which exists between the modern science of art and what passed for the science of art in the eighteenth century—in the writings, examples to cite only English, of Hogarth, Richardson and Reynolds—is almost total. It seems even more distinct than the difference between the arts themselves.

REYNOLDS AND THE GRAND MANNER

The art of the eighteenth century, as represented by Reynolds and codified in his *Discourses*, is a most curious dead-end in human development. Until the second half of the eighteenth century we can say that every period had its style, however obscure and however unworthy. But after this time the spirit of man apparently ceased to express itself in direct and original modes; it began instead to seek conformity with previous modes of expression: and so we get that series of revivals of style—the neo-Gothic, the neo-classic, the debased eclecticism of the Great Exhibitions—ending with the end of the nineteenth century in a general bankruptcy of the academic tradition.

The seeds of the decay were inherent in that secondary but finally predominant aspect of the Renaissance known as The Classical Revival. How far the ideals of the Classical Revival conform to the principles and practice of the artists of ancient Greece I will not attempt to estimate; but we may say that that aspect of Greek art which emphasized its intellectual or rational structure was seized on and made the canon of all aesthetic expression. 'There is (in Greek art) an almost metaphysical belief that beauty and the ideal type for sculptural representation are characterized by an almost supersensual, because intellectual and mathematical, structure.'[1] This notion of a canon of beauty, a type-form which should satisfy the reason in its quest for perfection, is the dominant characteristic of the whole classical tradition. When most justified (by the judgement of successive ages—a pragmatic test, I admit) this ideal reconciles the vitality of organic life, especially as represented by the human form, with the stability and universality of an intellectual concept. Natural facts are given a rational interpretation; the organic is lifted to the plane of the intellect; the vital seeks

[1] Rhys Carpenter: *The Esthetic Basis of Greek Art* (1921).

[22]

a point of equilibrium in physical law. But the virtue of an equilibrium is that it is easily upset: the thrill it communicates comes from its delicate tension. It was inevitable that the eighteenth century, with the gradual triumph of the Cartesian philosophy and the consequent degradation of instinct and imagination, should overweight the balance on the side of reason. And precisely *that* eventuality is fatal to the existence of art. Art may flourish in a rank and barbaric manner from an excess of animal vitality; but it withers and dies in the arid excesses of reason. And it is because, not for the first time in the history of man, reason became predominant in the philosophy of art, that art in the eighteenth century suffered such a complete eclipse.

The obsequies are, appropriately enough, celebrated with pomp and circumstance in the *Discourses* of Sir Joshua Reynolds; there the classical ideal is finally devitalized in the doctrine of the Grand Manner, or the Great Style. We shall best realize the distance modern art has travelled if we take this style as our point of departure. But it is not easy, as Reynolds himself realized, to define in what the Great Style consists; and Reynolds's own training had been too empirical for him to acquiesce in the notion that taste or genius could be taught by rules. 'Experience is all in all,' he said, 'but it is not everyone who profits by experience; and most people err, not so much from want of capacity to find their object, as from not knowing what object to pursue. . . . The power of discovering what is deformed in Nature, or, in other words, what is particular and uncommon, can be acquired only by experience; and the whole beauty and grandeur of Art consists . . . in being able to get above all singular forms, local customs, particularities, and details of every kind. All the objects which are exhibited to our view by Nature, upon close examination will be found to have their blemishes and defects. The most beautiful forms have something about them like weakness, minuteness, or imperfection. But it is not every eye that perceives these blemishes. It must be an eye long used to the contemplation and comparison of these forms. The Painter who aims at the greatest style . . . corrects Nature by herself, her imperfect state by her more perfect. His eye being enabled to distinguish the accidental deficiencies, excrescences, and deformities of things, from their general figures, *he makes out an abstract idea* of their forms more perfect than any one original. . . . This idea of the perfect state of Nature, which the artist calls the Ideal beauty, is the great leading principle by which works of genius are conducted.'[1]

Here we have the final formulation of the classical doctrine in art, and this final formulation does not differ essentially from that of Dryden at the end of the seventeenth century, or, for that matter, from that of Alberti in the fifteenth century. Common to them all is the notion that the artist 'makes out an abstract idea'; and that is the feature of the classical ideal to be kept in mind for purposes of contrast with the emergence of a new ideal. Further, the classical ideal is a static ideal, an ideal based on the *status quo* of a particular civilization, that civilization established in Greece and continued in Mediterranean Europe until the present day.

VICO AND THE RISE OF THE GENETIC CONCEPT OF ART

If I were to select a single word to characterize the opposing ideal which already in the eighteenth century had made its obscure appearance, that word would be *genetic*. And if I were to select a single name as the originator of this ideal, that name would be *Vico*. Within two years of Reynolds's birth, there was published in Italy the *Scienza Nuova* of Giambattista Vico, a work which, though its title makes a claim for novelty, was in effect a return to the principles and methods of the Scholastic philosophy, which in their turn were based on the principles and methods of Aristotle. This

[1] The Third Discourse (delivered December 14, 1770).

[24]

'new science' involved a conception of society as a developing organism, and Vico's aim, as it concerns us now, was to determine the place of art in the history of such an organism. This led him to the formulation of a theory of poetry totally distinct from the prevailing classical ideal, and distinct, therefore, from those principles of poetry which the seventeenth century regarded as for all times 'laid down by Plato and confirmed by Aristotle'. Vico identifies poetry with the primitive phase in the history of man: poetry is the first form of history, it is the metaphysic of man whilst he is still living in a direct sensuous relation to his environment, before he has learned to form universals and to reflect. Imagination is clearly differentiated from intellect, and all forms of poetic activity are shown to depend on the imagination; in civilized epochs poetry can only be written by those who have the capacity to suspend the operation of the intellect, to put the mind in fetters and to return to the unreflecting mode of thought characteristic of the childhood of the race.

I must not expatiate too much on Vico's theory of poetry, though I believe it to be of profound significance: I can only refer to Croce's exposition of the subject, to Vico himself, and throw out the prediction that we are going to hear a great deal more about Vico in the immediate[1] future, and that, in short, his theories are going to play a predominant part in the development of modern criticism. Meanwhile I want to emphasize the significance of the method employed by Vico: the return to origins. His theory is based on a study of mythology and particularly of Homer. That is what I mean by the *genetic* method—a method that studies art in relation to its origins, its history and distribution—in brief, the

---

[1] This word was too optimistic in 1933. But translations of Vico's works have been proceeding and several critical studies have been published, with the result that Vico's importance is now fully realized. His main work, *La Scienza Nuova Seconda*, has appeared in a translation by T. G. Bergin and U. H. Fisch (Cornell Univ. Press, 1948), and A. R. Caponigri has written an excellent study of Vico's theory of history, *Time and Idea* (London, 1953).

[25]

empirical method itself. The whole of the modern tradition in art is a direct result of such an approach to art: art no longer conceived as a rational ideal, a painful striving towards an intellectual perfection; but art conceived as a stage in the ideal history of mankind, as a pre-logical mode of expression, as something necessary and inevitable and organic, the language of the Heroic age, the expression of imaginative heroism in the life of the artist in any age.

METAPHYSICAL AESTHETICS

The next name I would like to mention is that of *Herder*, though I ought to refer in passing to his master Baumgarten, who has perhaps gained a rather fictitious importance by inventing the name *aesthetics*, and by making the first attempt to claim the subject as a science. He defined aesthetics as 'the science of sensuous knowledge', and gave birth to that great school of metaphysical aesthetic represented by Kant and Hegel—an idealistic, aprioristic approach to our subject which has little relevance to our practical enquiry. It cannot be said that the course of art has in any way been influenced by the *Critique of Judgment*. But Herder, unlike Kant but like Vico, went back to the sources, to objective things, to primitive poetry and folk-song, and his conclusions are the same as Vico's. Again it is the method that is significant: it was applied in the main to the study of language and poetry, but its relevance to the visual or plastic arts was still unobserved.

After Kant the world, as Jean Paul Richter said, swarmed with aestheticians. I have never been able to believe that the idealistic conception of art, developed on the basis of Kant's aesthetic by writers like Fichte and Schelling, and given a more popular romantic expression by poets like Richter and Novalis, is worth the time that would be involved in mastering its mysteries. It consists mainly of a discussion of abstract categories like imagination and fancy, form and idea, and these are rarely, if ever, related to ob-

[26]

jective works of art. There is no critical method involved, no cor-relation of the historical facts. To describe the Homeric epic, as Schelling does, as 'the very identity conditioning the foundation of history in the Absolute', is a deplorable departure from the pre-cision of Vico's Homeric criticism. I do not wish this to be con-strued as a reflection on philosophy in general, for philosophy properly conceived is the highest of all mental disciplines; but science is prior to philosophy, and a science of art must establish its facts before a philosophy of art can make use of them. Philo-sophers have in general ignored the possibility of a science of art and have proceeded on *a priori* assumptions as to its nature.

Exceptions must be made of Schiller and Hegel. Friedrich Schiller's Letters *Über die Ästhetische Erziehung des Menschen*[1] were published in 1793, and are perhaps the most important contribu-tion to aesthetic philosophy between Plato and Croce. Their main thesis is, indeed, a reaffirmation of what I have elsewhere called 'Plato's most passionate ideal', the thesis that art should be the basis of education. Schiller argued that the development of the aesthetic sensibility was the essential basis for the development of reason and morality—that it was the formative exercise, so to speak, for the education of those faculties that enable man, not only to introduce some order into his sensuous experience, but also to effect that balance between instinct and reason upon which the harmony of life no less than the vitality of art absolutely depends. It cannot be said that Schiller's aesthetic philosophy had any immediate in-fluence on the origins of the modern movement in art, but as Croce said, to Schiller belongs the great merit of having opposed the sub-jective idealism of Kant and of having made the attempt to surpass it. With Schelling he is the main precursor of the Romantic move-ment in art and literature, and in essentials we are still part of that movement.

[1] Trans. by Reginald Snell: *On the Aesthetic Education of Man*, Lon-don, 1954.

[27]

Hegel gives the final and most definitive expression to an ideal-istic philosophy of art. Like Schiller, he recognized the basic nature of the aesthetic phase in human development, but he treated it as a phase that had to be superseded by the 'higher' phases of religion and philosophy. Beauty is Truth, Truth Beauty, but merely in the sense that the beautiful is the sensible appearance of the Idea. Nevertheless, Hegel shows throughout his *Philosophy of Fine Art* a real sensibility towards all forms of art—a sensibility often in ad-vance of his time. I might instance, as examples of his acuity, his defence of the librettos of Mozart's operas; his perception that the superiority of Dante's epic over all other epics was due to the ele-ment of sympathy; and, in the sphere of the plastic arts, a passage like the following, which shows a habit of accurate observation:

'It is, therefore, *colour*, and the art of colouring, which make the painter a painter. We dwell with pleasure, no doubt, on the draw-ing, and exceptionally so on the study or sketch, as on that which pre-eminently betrays the quality of genius; but however rich with invention and imagination, with whatever directness the soul of an artist may assert itself in such studies by reason of the more trans-parent and mobile shell of their form, yet the fact remains that to be painting we must have colour, if the work is not to continue abstract from the point of view of its sensuous material in the vital individuality and articulation of its objects. We must, however, at the same time admit that drawings and dry point drawings from the hand of great masters such as Raphael and Albrecht Dürer are of real importance. In fact from a certain point of view we may say that it is just these hand drawings which carry with them the finest interest. We find here the wonderful result that the entire spirit of the master is expressed directly in such manual facility, a facility which places with the greatest ease, in instantaneous work, without any preliminary essays, the essential substance of the master's con-ception. The border drawings of Dürer, for example, in the Prayer-book of the Munich library, are of indescribable ideality and freedom. Idea and execution appear in such a case to be one and the same thing, whereas in finished pictures we cannot avoid the sense that the consummate result is only secured after repeated over-paintings, a continuous process of advance and finish.'[1]

But all Hegel's experience of art was of no avail against the over-ruling necessities of his system, for, as Croce has pointed out, 'the principles of Hegel's system are at bottom rationalistic and hostile to religion, and hostile no less to art.' Art for Hegel was only a stage, and a lower stage, in the progress of the mind towards truth. Art can represent truth in sensible form only, but, he thought, we have passed beyond the stage when the mind can be satisfied with such representations. The absolute must now be apprehended by the spirit, that is to say, by philosophy, and art must be discarded like the toys of a childhood we have outgrown. Obviously, a philo-sopher who puts art so firmly in the past cannot be of use to anyone who is trying to find a philosophy of art in the present.

For similar reasons we shall pass by the names of Schopenhauer, Herbart and Schleiermacher; in spite of the many brilliant things they have to say about art as a general concept, they are all engaged in the philosophical game of system-building, and we feel that their theories of art have no essential connection with works of art. Fundamentally they are neither critically nor historically minded: they accept the taste and cultural traditions of their own time as infallible and are content to quote as illustrations a few hackneyed types like the Apollo of the Belvedere. The famous philologist, Wilhelm von Humboldt, is a much more significant figure. His specifically aesthetic works seem to be of no great originality, being mere commentaries on the classical canons: but his main work is based on an objective study of language and in this field he came to exactly the same conclusions as Vico—that language, for example, is a product of the struggle to reach an intuition of things, that

---

[1] *The Philosophy of Fine Art* by G. W. F. Hegel. Trans. by F. P. B. Osmaston. 4 vols ,1920. Vol. iii, p. 275.

poetry precedes prose and gives us reality in its sensible appearance. But he never seems to have thought of applying this same objective method to the plastic arts, confining himself to vague analogies and comparisons.

THE EMPIRICAL APPROACH

This long and increasingly complicated movement of *a priori* aesthetics continued far past the middle of the nineteenth century, but its very excesses produced a reaction. The first to react were the positivists—Herbert Spencer and Grant Allen in England, and Taine in France—but in its first violence this reaction was extremely crude: we come down from the clouds but we do not find ourselves in the region of art. I defy anyone to associate aesthetic sensibility with the mentality of Herbert Spencer. But it is a different matter with Gustav Theodor Fechner, whose *Vorschule der Ästhetik* was first published in 1876. Fechner is the real founder of the modern science of art, the first philosopher to study art 'von unten', to base an aesthetic on an empirical or inductive study of works of art. He inaugurated experimental methods that are still being pursued in psychological laboratories all over the world, in spite of Croce's contemptuous dismissal of them as 'a pastime or hobby neither more nor less important than playing Patience or collecting stamps'. Regarded separately these methods may often seem ridiculous enough and irrelevant; but in their aggregate, and as summarized, for example, in the survey made by O. Külpe,[1] there can be no doubt that they have taught us a lot about the physical character of objects commonly accepted as beautiful, and a lot about the psychological reactions of various types of people to such objects. It is the philosopher's own fault if he is not able to assimilate such facts into his general theory of art.

I attach much more importance to the type of empirical study

[1] *Der gegenwärtige Stand der experimentellen Ästhetik* (1906).

represented by names like Gottfried Semper, Konrad Fiedler, and Ernst Grosse. Semper is the historical materialist in the sphere of art; he accepts (and this in itself is an original step for which he cannot be given too much credit) the whole evidence presented by works of art surviving from any epoch and asks: what are the universal and typical forms which we can discern in all this multiplicity? He surveys all his material and points out the recurring forms and motives; he then asks whether these are determined by the purpose which the object has to serve, the material from which it is made, or the nature of the tools and technical methods used in its making. Semper's principal work[1] appeared in 1860 and has continued to exercise considerable influence, not only on direct disciples in the method like Alois Riegl in his study of late Roman art,[2] but on artists (the present-day emphasis on the doctrine that the artist must respect the nature of his material derives directly from it) and on the arrangement of museums. There is no doubt that Semper's method is an extremely fertile one, and when it is used, as he used it, with unfailing sensibility and soundness, it must lead to a much better comprehension of the nature of the artistic activity in man, and the conditions which determine its forms throughout history—the conditions, we might add, which are determining its forms to-day.

Semper's ideas have been developed with great subtlety and intelligence by Konrad Fiedler, an aesthetician who is sadly neglected in England and grossly under-rated by writers like Croce. Fiedler develops Riegl's idea that art is the will creative in the terms of a material: the artist considers his material and solves, not the technical problem of representation, but the formal problem of expression. 'The artist (he says) is not differentiated from other people by

[1] *Der Stil in den technischen und tektonischen Künsten oder praktische Ästhetik*, 1860.
[2] *Spätrömische Kunstindustrie*. Vienna, 1927. Riegl, however, developed a quasi-mystical doctrine of the 'will to art' hardly consistent with Semper's objectivity.

any special perceptive faculty enabling him to perceive more or with greater intensity, or endowing his eye with any special power of selecting, collecting, transforming, ennobling or illuminating; but rather by his peculiar gift of being able to pass immediately from perception to intuitive expression; his relation to nature is not perceptive, but expressive'—and expressive, we might add, in tangible and sensible objects, objects which conform to their material essence. The artist speaks in stone, in wood, in bronze, in colour, just as the poet speaks in words: the artist makes thought visible, without the intermediary of verbal concepts. This is a very significant theory, one of the main theories underlying the practice of contemporary artists.[1] Fiedler, who was active in the eighties and nineties of the last century, was in close contact with the most original artists of his day—with Hans von Marées and Adolf von Hildebrand—and his doctrine, with its striking insistence on the necessity of originality (for there is no proper artistic activity in the use of conventional forms, as there would be no proper poetic expression in the use of conventional metaphors), is peculiarly relevant to our present purpose. Fiedler, in fact, was ready to admit that the new and significant in art can only arise out of direct opposition to the past; and in relation to modern architecture, for example, he would have insisted on the necessity of thinking within the terms of the materials, steel and concrete, to the exclusion of all ideas derived from the utilization of outmoded materials like wood and stone.

The third name I mentioned as particularly significant in the foundation of an aesthetic of modern art was that of Ernst Grosse. In 1894, whilst still in his twenties, he published his first book, *Die Anfänge der Kunst* (The Beginnings of Art). Grosse, more decisively than anyone else, breaks away from the idea that art is

---

[1] It has been further developed by Henri Focillon in *The Life of Forms in Art* (Trans. by C. Beecher Hogan and George Kubler. Yale Univ. Press, 1942), one of the most precise and beautiful works in the realm of aesthetics.

confined to the products of the Graeco-Roman tradition, and insists on the science of art incorporating, in the manner of any other humanistic science, the whole genesis and scope of the artistic activity. And just as science in general, in so far as it is concerned with organic life, is almost inconceivable on any but a genetic and evolutionary basis, so this facet of human life must be studied in its origins and development. Thus began that research into prehistoric and primitive art which is still progressing, and which, by bringing to our attention the works of primitive and prehistoric peoples, and pointing out their aesthetic significance, has been one of the most powerful influences in modern art. For in primitive art we see so clearly, what is so difficult to perceive in the complex products of highly cultured civilizations—the directly expressive quality of the artist's vision, its objectification in solid shapes.

THE SIGNIFICANCE OF PRIMITIVE ART

Parallel to this line of approach, and on the principle that ontogenesis repeats phylogenesis, we have had a serious study of the art of children, culminating in the comparatively recent works of Bühler, Wulff, Eng and Lowenfeld. I shall say no more about it than that it has fully confirmed the general validity of the genetic method in aesthetics, and again, by drawing attention to the positive qualities of children's art, has had a direct influence on the practice of modern artists—there has been a deliberate attempt to reach back to the naivety and fresh simplicity of the childlike outlook—a retrograde step, of course, if you regard 'the march of intellect' with complacency or satisfaction.[1] It is not claimed that the art of savages, prehistoric men and children can be given the same value as the art of civilized men: in the humanistic scale of values,

[1] I have dealt fully with this aspect of the subject in *Education Through Art* (London: new edition 1953).

such art is almost negligible. But our present enquiry is concerned, not with the problem of values, but with the nature and development of art, and from this point of view it is impossible to exaggerate the significance of primitive art. The virtue of a plant is in its seed: its form is implicit in its first shoot. We can learn more of the essential nature of art from its earliest manifestations in primitive man (and in children) than from its intellectual elaboration in great periods of culture. For in its later stages art is overlaid by modes of life and manners that are not of its essence. Primitive man and the child do not distinguish in our ratiocinative manner between the real and ideal. Art for them is perhaps not so disinterested: it is not extraneous and complementary to life, but an intensification of life: a stirring of the pulse, a heightening of the heart's beat, a tautening of the muscles, a necessary and exigent mode of expression. Art, indeed, is regarded by primitive man as of such practical importance that its use is socialized; an artist for art's sake would probably be killed as a dangerous devil, but an artist for the community's sake becomes priest and king, for he is the maker of magic, the voice of the spirits, the inspired oracle, the intermediary through whom the tribe secures fertility for their crops or success for their hunters. His hand is veritably the hand of God.

Art from this point of view, let us frankly admit, has nothing to do with polite culture or intelligence. In its origins it is an exercise or activity of the senses, the plastic expression of elementary intuitions. As such, it is not the possession of one people, but is diffused over the whole world. But in its creative aspect it is a limited activity —that is to say, it is confined to special individuals who have special gifts or skills—powers not of feeling or of thought—but of expression, or reification. With these powers, the favoured individual can appeal to the aesthetic sensibility of the whole community. Art is therefore closely related to skill—not only because all visual or plastic arts depend on learning the use of some tool, but also be-

[34]

cause they make use of the ability to fashion objects to the will, to the heart's desire. But art is more than skill, because skill is purely functional. Art begins where function ends: it is a refinement on function, though it should not interfere with function. Where functional forms are equal in operative efficiency, there is still room for the aesthetic sensibility to make a choice—to say that one spearhead is *more beautiful* than another, one axe *more beautiful* than another. And this brings us down to the root-problem of aesthetics —what do we imply by this preference? That one shape is more pleasing than another—but why? If it had done nothing else, the genetic method in aesthetics would have justified itself by finally isolating this question. In order to answer it, another method was necessary—the psychological method. It is not possible to explain the pleasure or satisfaction we derive from the formal elements in art until we have laid bare the physiology of instinctive responses, explained the part played by pattern in the stimulation of visual acuteness, the relation of rhythm to bodily and perhaps (as the Chinese would have us believe) to cosmic movements, the unconscious appeal of representational and non-representational symbols, the emotive effect of pure colours and tones, and so on.

THE PSYCHOLOGY OF ART, THE RECEPTIVE ASPECT

To give any adequate account of modern psychological theories of art is beyond the scope of this essay. We owe the establishment of a scientific psychology of art mainly to four Germans—Karl Groos, Theodor Lipps, J. Volkelt, and Max Dessoir—and their enquiries revolve for the most part round what is known as the theory of Einfühlung, or *empathy*. This theory tends to become so generalized that it loses a good deal of its specific application to works of art. Primarily it is a theory of aesthetic appreciation, in contrast to the theories which we have just been considering, which

[35]

were more concerned with the object and the conditions of its creation. It is a theory which finds the explanation of aesthetic pleasure
in the nature of the sympathetic relation established between the
spectator and the work of art. This is revealed as no mere fellow-
feeling, of feeling *with*, but rather a form of imaginative identification of the self with the object, a feeling *into*. It is an immediate,
direct, intuitive relation of perception to the *form* of the object. Lipps,
who is the classical exponent of the theory, describes it in this way:

'The object of sympathy is our objectified ego, transposed into
others and therefore discovered in them. We feel ourselves in others
and we feel others in ourselves. In others, or by means of them, we
feel ourselves happy, free, enlarged, elevated, or the contrary of all
these. The aesthetic feeling of sympathy is not a mere mode of
aesthetic enjoyment, it is that enjoyment itself. All aesthetic enjoyment is founded, in the last analysis, singly and wholly upon sympathy: even that caused by geometrical, architectonic, and other
abstract lines and forms.'

But it would be an abuse of the word to describe the latter mode
of feeling as sympathy: we do not necessarily humanize the rising
column or the graceful vase which we contemplate: we feel into
its shape, conform to it, and react to its limits, its mass, its rhyth-
mic convolution; and so we invent the word *empathy*. Further, it is
possible to say that empathy is a vitally different thing according as
the object of contemplation is human, organic, or abstract; Lipps
himself distinguishes between simple and symbolic empathy. What
I want to make clear, and I think my statement is warranted by
Lipps and Volkelt, is that the initial stage in this process is not one
of feeling: it is not merely a sentimental association of the self with
the object. There is a direct intuitive awareness of form, an unconscious identification, and the specifically aesthetic *feeling* follows.
This is made particularly clear by certain types of contemporary
abstract art.

We must, in fact, distinguish three stages in the complete aesthe-

[36]

tic experience before a work of art: (1) the immediate perception or apprehension of the object, (2) the reaction of the affective system to the form of the apprehended object, and (3) the reaction of the spectator's mind to the conceptual nature of the object, to the 'content', that is to say, of the work of art, and to all its secondary associations.

THE CREATIVE ASPECT

The creative aspect of art, according to this theory, is a more complicated process. Here I do not propose to follow any particular lead, but I think the general theory of the psychological school I have mentioned would allow us to distinguish the following stages of the creative process in the visual arts: they correspond very closely with the stages in other arts, such as poetry and music:

1. There is first a predisposing emotional mood, a state of readiness or awareness, perhaps a sense of the momentary availability of the unconscious levels of the mind.

2. Whilst he is in this state there come to the artist the first premonitions of a symbol, or thought to be expressed, not in words, but in visible and tangible material shape—perhaps 'this landscape', 'this dish of fruit', perhaps only an abstract adumbration of planes and masses.

3. Then, as a third step, we have the mental elaboration of this symbol, the introduction or selection of images which the mind intuitively associates with the symbol, the determination of the emotional value or pressure of the images.

4. Next the artist seeks an appropriate method, including an appropriate material, by means of which he can represent the symbol.

5. Finally, there is the actual technical process of translating the mental perception into objective form—a process during which the original symbol may receive considerable modifications.

It should be observed, however, that what we in this psychological manner analyse into five consecutive and distinct stages, in actual practice takes place as an integral and inseparable activity. Moreover, the artist does not necessarily always begin at the beginning, with a vague emotional mood. He may begin at almost any stage and go backwards before going forwards—he may, and very often does, begin with the material, paint or stone, and from a concentration on this, and perhaps from a playful preliminary activity with his tools, he induces the preliminary mood. But fundamental to all exact psychology of the creative process is the notion that art is the expression through the senses of states of intuition, perception or emotion, *peculiar to the individual*. Nowhere, in the modern psychology of art, will you find any justification for the notion that art is primarily an intellectual activity concerned with the formulation of absolute ideas or ideal types. That art has been and still is occupied with human and spiritual values, the psychologist is willing to admit; but these have nothing to do with the nature of the aesthetic process itself. One may speak of aesthetic values but they are distinct from values in ethics, sociology, religion or philosophy. Art is concerned with sentience, with visual cognition, with symbolization, but never with intellection, generalization or judgement. On that dogma, supported as it is by the whole force of the modern science of art, the practice of contemporary art stands or falls.

THE PRESENT PHILOSOPHY OF ART

It is natural to ask, in conclusion, whether the very diverse speculations and discoveries of the modern science of art which I have so cursorily surveyed, have received any integration within a modern system of philosophy. No contemporary philosopher can now safely neglect this sphere of the human spirit, but it is to be doubted whether any one since Hegel has given it an adequate or just place within a unified view of the universe. Croce, of course,

[38]

has made the attempt, but it is an attempt which rests on a rejection of the evidence of the empirical and psychological approach I have described, and which resorts instead to a species of solipsism that attempts to identify aesthetics and linguistics. It is the last flicker of a defunct idealism, and has to a large extent been superseded by more empirical approaches based on the study of language and myth, and above all on the psychology of the artist. It has become increasingly evident that art has an important biological and sociological function in the life of man. In this respect the work of Henri Bergson has considerable significance. It is true that Bergson never wrote a work devoted specifically to aesthetics: we are left to gather together for ourselves the incidental wisdom on this subject which lies scattered through his various books. As an example of this wisdom, and as a definition of art which seems to me to be reconcilable, not only with the vast range of artistic expression in the past and in our present time, but also with the objective theories of art which I have described, I would like to quote a passage from his book on *Laughter*:

'From time to time, in a fit of absent-mindedness, nature raises up souls that are more detached from life. Not with that intentional, logical, systematical detachment—the result of reflection and philosophy, but rather with a natural detachment, one innate in the structure of sense or consciousness, which at once reveals itself by a virginal manner, so to speak, of seeing, hearing, or thinking. . . .

'One man applies himself to colours and forms, and since he loves colour for colour and form for form, since he perceives them for their sake and not for his own, it is the inner life of things that he sees appearing through their forms and colours. Little by little he insinuates it into our own perception, baffled though we may be at the outset. For a few moments at least, he diverts us from the prejudices of form and colour that come between ourselves and reality. And thus he realizes the loftiest ambition of art, which here

[39]

consists in revealing to us nature. Others, again, retire within themselves. Beneath the thousand rudimentary actions which are the outward and visible signs of an emotion, behind the common-place, conventional expression that both reveals and conceals an individual mental state, it is the emotion, the original mood, to which they attain in its undefiled essence. And then, to induce us to make the same effort ourselves, they contrive to make us see something of what they have seen: by rhythmical arrangement of words, which thus become organized and animated with a life of their own, they tell us—or rather suggest—things that speech was not calculated to express. Others delve yet deeper still. Beneath these joys and sorrows which can, at a pinch, be translated into language, they grasp something that has nothing in common with language, certain rhythms of life and breath that are closer to man than his inmost feelings, being the living law—varying with each individual—of his enthusiasm and despair, his hopes and regrets. By setting free and emphasizing this music, they force it upon our attention; they compel us, willy-nilly, to fall in with it, like passers-by who join in a dance. And thus they impel us to set in motion, in the depths of our being, some secret chord which was only waiting to thrill. . . .'[1]

There are many terms in such a statement that would need defining in an exact aesthetic, but alike in the loftiness of its conception and the truth of its observation, these words adequately summarize that revolution in thought which has accompanied and which sanctions the revolution in contemporary art.

After Bergson by far the most significant philosopher in this field (though again not specifically a philosopher of art) has been Ernst Cassirer (1874-1945). Cassirer's most important work, from our point of view, is his *Philosophy of Symbolic Forms*[2] in which he

---

[1] *Laughter* (1900) by Henri Bergson. Trans. by C. Brereton and F. Rothwell, London and New York, 1911.

[2] The original edition in German was published in 3 vols. 1923 and 1929. A translation by Ralph Manheim has been published by the Yale Univ. Press, 1953, 1955, 1957.

takes up Kant's philosophy of form and develops it into a phenom-
enology of culture, using for this purpose the accumulated science
of a century's research into the origins of language and myth. What
man achieves in the course of his historical development is 'the objectification, the intuition of himself, in and through the theoretical,
aesthetic, and ethical form which he gives to his existence. This is
exhibited even in the very first promptings of human speech and it
is unfolded and developed in rich and many-sided forms in poetry,
in the fine arts, in religious consciousness, in philosophical concepts.
Art is for the first time clearly conceived, not as the mere reproduction of a ready-made, given reality, but as the discovery of reality,
which discovery is communicated in symbolic form. The limiting
concept of beauty is discarded. Art, as Goethe had said, is formative
long before it is beautiful; it gives form to feelings that are other-
wise obscure or inchoate, and that is its main biological and cultural
function. Art is 'an interpretation of reality—not by concepts but
by intuitions; not through the medium of thought but through that
of sensuous forms'.[1]

Cassirer is, of course, a product of the German idealist tradition
in philosophy, but he corrects this tradition in a vital matter. 'The
real subject of art', he points out, 'is not the metaphysical Infinite
of Schelling, nor is it the Absolute of Hegel. It is to be sought in
certain fundamental structural elements of our sense experience
itself—in lines, design, in architectural, musical forms. These elements are, so to speak, omnipresent. Free of all mystery, they are
patent and unconcealed; they are visible, audible, tangible'.[2]

Cassirer's philosophy of symbolic forms has been applied more
specifically to art by Susanne K. Langer who also makes use of the
many scattered insights into the subject for which Whitehead was

---

[1] *An Essay on Man*, Doubleday Anchor Books (1953), p. 188. The sec-
tion on 'Art' in this *Introduction to a Philosophy of Human Culture* is the
best and most accessible summary of Cassirer's philosophy of art.
[2] Op. cit., p. 201.

responsible.[1] With Cassirer and Langer the philosophy of art attains a reasonably convincing and definitive form, and one can now see that the whole development of a modern philosophy of art, beginning with Vico and Kant, receiving decisive contributions from Rousseau and Goethe, has been guided step by step by the development of art itself. In art and in philosophy there is the gradual realization of the formative and transformative nature of the artistic activity, and of its independent cognitive status. These developments together constitute the Romantic Movement, and though, as we shall see, there are certain aspects of modern art that are anti-romantic or classicist in intention, they but illustrate the limitations of any term that would attempt to characterize the creative imagination of man. Art is indeed the discovery and establishment of a new world of forms, and form is rational; but art is a continual transformation of form by forces that are vital and irrational.

[1] *Philosophy in a New Key*, Harvard Univ. Press, 1942; *Feeling and Form*, New York, 1953.

Chapter II

FROM SCIENCE TO SYMBOLISM

THE BREAK-UP OF THE ACADEMIC TRADITION

There is one general aspect of contemporary art about which everyone is agreed. I mean its complexity. Nobody would be bold enough to select one particular school or tradition and say: this is the type of modern art, all the rest is in some manner derivative or false. At other times, even down to the end of the last century, there has been a certain unity in the development of art, so that historians have been able to trace from generation to generation a coherent evolution of style. But where, in the immediate ancestry of modern art, shall we find the forebears of Picasso, Paul Klee, Max Ernst, and many of the other artists whose diverse work might be mentioned? There seems to be a definite break in the historical development of the artistic faculty.

It might be possible to draw some parallel between this condition of the arts and the general social conditions of our civilization. The complexity of styles in art, the apparent discontinuity in their development, is not greater than the complexity of what we might well call styles in morals, religion and social economics. Everywhere there is the same lack of unity, the same absence of authority, the same break with tradition. There will not be wanting critics who will try to find a causal chain linking all aspects of this confusion—beginning, as is the fashion, with economic

[43]

conditions, and deducing from their chaos, the chaos of the arts and other cultural manifestations of our time.

GENERAL CHARACTER OF THE REVOLUTION

There have been revolutions in the history of art before to-day. There is a revolution with every new generation, and periodically, every century or so, we get a wider or a deeper change of sensibility which is recognized as a period—the Trecento, the Quattro Cento, the Baroque, the Rococo, the Romantic, the Impressionist and so on. But I do think we can already discern a difference of kind in the contemporary revolution: it is not so much a revolution, which implies a turning-over, even a turning-back, but rather a break-up, a devolution, some would say a dissolution. Its character is catastrophic. Historical revolutions begin as isolated ferments, which gradually spread until they infect, transform, infuse the whole body of a civilization. But now we have rather the birth of a new body, or bodies, distinct in character and incapable of fusion with the old body. The traditional art of the Renaissance, the art of Humanism, in spite of all its periodical changes, remains one tradition right down to the Impressionist and even to the Post-Impressionist schools. That tradition, now crystallized as contemporary academic art, remains constant and uncontaminated; and however much we may rail against it, it does not die, and judging by the popular and official support given to it, it does not seem to decay. It thrives in its distinct sphere, and I think it will continue to thrive because fundamentally it satisfies social needs quite distinct from those satisfied by that other type of art which we call specifically 'modern'. It is to the diversity of the human spirit, and with the realization that this diversity can be diversely expressed, that we must look for an explanation of the vitality and of the validity of the modern movement.

[44]

PAUL KLEE
Sun and Moon Flowers

I do not wish to imply that the human spirit is more diverse to-day than at any other historical period. Nor do I wish to imply that we know more about the human spirit to-day than was known in the day of, say, Aristotle or at any time since. What I do feel as true of our own time is that we have in some way telescoped our past development so that the human spirit, which in the past has expressed itself, or some predominant aspect of itself, diversely at different times, now expresses the same diversity, without any stress on any particular aspect, at one and the same time. The diversity of modern art is discontinuous, and cannot be made to fit into any one theoretical concept; but we can find a parallel for most of its aspects in the history of art. The novelty is, that these aspects, these concepts of art, have never before existed side by side, within one another, at one and the same time. Nevertheless, I think it is possible that we have added just one new concept to the previously existing ones, as I shall try to show in later chapters.

THE ACADEMIC TRADITION
'WHAT THE EYE SEES'

The main tradition of European painting, that tradition which for convenience I shall call *academic*, begins in the fourteenth century. Without attaching too much importance to any individual, like Giotto, we may say without much fear of contradiction that it begins with the desire to reproduce in some way exactly what the eye sees. 'It was required of the artist', as Roger Fry once so well expressed it, 'not only that his imagery should appeal to the emotions by its rhythm, but that it should conform to the appearance of the actual world. Its texture had to be as continuous and unbroken as that of the visible scene, a condition which . . . was not enforced on the artists of China. That continuity of texture might be obtained in two ways, either by an accurate imitation of an actual scene or by constructing a picture according to those optical laws to which

[45]

our vision inevitably conforms. The former, the empirical method, was used in Northern Europe by Flemish artists, the latter, the scientific, was worked out in Italy, especially by the Florentines, who first discovered the optical laws of appearance.'[1] Here already, within a general description of the academic tradition, we have two methods indicated, the *empirical* and the *scientific*, and these two terms will describe the content of contemporary academic art. As its name implies, the empirical method succeeds, by whatever technical deftness it can devise, in giving an illusion of direct, visual experience. It is the imitative method in all its naivety, and just because it is imitative, and has no other aim beyond the reproduction of appearances, it is of little theoretical interest. We may be satisfied with this type of art: we may demand of the artist an exact record of the record given by the physiological mechanism of his sight. If so, all that we can demand of the artist is in its essence mechanical. He must be a perfect machine. The rest is in the subject painted, and about that we may have our opinions, our sentiments, even our emotions; but they have nothing to do with the working of the machine. Thus the empirical method in painting, like the same method in philosophy, ends in materialism: it is a mechanistic theory of art.

WHAT *DOES* THE EYE SEE?

The other method is the empirical method submitted to scientific scepticism. Instead of reproducing quite innocently what he imagines the eye to see, the painter asks himself: But what exactly does my eye see? He is no longer content with the illusion, empirically reached by technical deftness. He must analyse what the eye sees, and then build up a chart, a diagram, that will bear a verifiable

[1] *An Outline of Modern Knowledge.* Ed. by Dr. William Rose, London, 1931, p. 949. By 'empirical' Fry means the method of trial and error. 'Pragmatic' might have been a more appropriate word.

relation to the object painted. At first he is concerned with the problem of translating on to a two-dimensional plane the three-dimensional nature of the field of vision: he is concerned, the artist like Uccello or Piero della Francesca, with theories of linear perspective. He works hand-in-hand with the mathematician or the geometrist. Then he realizes the importance of light and shade, of chiaroscuro, for the solution of his problem, and again he enlists the aid of the scientist. At a later stage he begins to realise that the outward appearance of objects depends on their inner structure: he becomes a geologist, to study the formation of rocks; a botanist, to study the forms of vegetation; an anatomist, to study the play of muscles, and the framework of bones. A typical artist of the Renaissance, like Leonardo da Vinci, was all of these things, but even Leonardo did not exhaust the application of science to art. He left comparatively untouched the all-important question of colour. But many scientists—Newton and Goethe, for example—had to work on this problem before the artist could make use of their results. Meanwhile an academic convention of colour sprang up which demanded above all a harmony or unity of tone-values on the canvas, a convention against which Constable was the first to revolt. Once Constable had shown that the colours in a painting could be as fresh and vivid as the colours in nature, the artist was set on a new scientific trend, which ended in the scientific or pseudo-scientific colour schemes of the impressionists like Seurat and Signac. I say 'ended' there, because for once science was applied too severely to art, and it was realized that analysis pushed too far ends by destroying the very aim of the scientific method in art, which is still to reproduce the appearance of the actual world. 'Continuity of texture' was no longer obtained by this means, and the scientific method itself became doubtful in principle.

[47]

A NEW CONCEPTION: SYMBOLISM

Perhaps this doubt would not have expanded into a revolt (it might have degenerated into despair) but for the incursion about the same time of new influences—particularly the influence of that method in art which was neither empirical nor scientific but which, during the whole of the period during which these methods were developing in Western Europe, continued its impassive course in the Far East. An art which renounced the desire to reproduce the appearance of the actual world—which, indeed, never conceived this aim, was suddenly 'discovered' by the stale-mated devotees of the scientific method. The influence, for example, of imported Japanese prints on the whole of the Post-Impressionist movement in France during the last quarter of the nineteenth century was out of all proportion to either the quality or quantity of these works of art. Men saw in a flash that painting could be something completely other than a reproduction of the appearance of the actual world— could be something perhaps only remotely like the appearance of the actual world. The empirical school, of course, were not particularly interested, and even the scientific school, among whom we may include even Cézanne and Van Gogh, were as a whole far too deeply committed to their professional technique to be capable of much change. But there existed in France at that time an amateur painter with no particular predilections or training who had just thrown up his post in a bank and even deserted his wife and family to devote himself to painting. He had no scientific or empirical prejudices, and submitted easily to the influence of oriental art: he had spent part of his childhood in a tropical country. This was Paul Gauguin, and though in some respects he was to continue to be an inefficient and even a sentimental painter, there is no doubt now that his influence was to be decisive for the future. In 1888, at Pont-Aven, he met another painter, Paul Sérusier. Sérusier has no great reputation as an artist, but he saw at once the freshness, the appeal and the force of Gauguin's work, and set about to formulate a theory to explain it.[1] Sérusier was logical, clear, systematic; he had a gift for abstract thought, and the theory he derived from the work and talk of Gauguin was soon seen to be distinct from the theories of Impressionism. At the time it received the not inept name of Symbolism, and it is probably only because the contemporary literary movement in France usurped this name that painting since Gauguin has not been labelled Symbolist.

This theory, ultimately sanctioned by Oriental art, but formulated by Sérusier[2] on the basis of Gauguin's work, was afterwards extended to include the work of Van Gogh. The aim of five centuries of European effort is openly abandoned. The actual appearance of the visible world is no longer of primary importance. The artist seeks something underneath appearances, some plastic symbol that will be more significant of reality than any exact reproduction can be. Perhaps this theory, so quietly formulated in the seclusion of a French village, did not seem so revolutionary at the time. But it opened the door to every development of modern art, to all the complexities which face us now. The whole difference between the modern movement in art and the tradition which had prevailed for five preceding centuries is expressed in this substitution of the symbolic for the descriptive as the aim of art. 'In painting', wrote Gauguin, 'one must search rather for suggestion than for description, as in music.'

THE THEORY OF SYMBOLIST ART

This aim, so simply formulated, is so important in its consequences that we must dwell on it a little, and test its validity. I have

[1] *A.B.C. de la peinture.* (Paris, 1921.)
[2] For the importance of Sérusier, see *Théories* by Maurice Denis (Paris, 4th edn. 1920), pp. 147–9, and *Les Arts Plastiques*, by Jacques Emile Blanche (Paris, 1931), p. 243.

already said that it is sanctioned by Oriental art in general, and unless we are to prescribe one art for the East, and one for the West, this evidence cannot be avoided. It is the mere commonplace, not only of Oriental decorative art, but even of such reproductive arts as figure-sculpture, landscape and portrait painting, that no attempt whatever is made to produce the illusion of the visible appearance of the actual object. There are some people who think that this is due to the poor Chinaman's inability to understand the elements of perspective and chiaroscuro. They seem capable of believing that an artistic culture which has lasted for five thousand years, a civilization which has reached the highest attainments in all spiritual spheres, remained obtusely ignorant in this matter of perspective drawing and reproductive verisimilitude generally. Unless we are to make all knowledge dependent on accidental causes, should we not rather conclude that our particular conventions of perspective and chiaroscuro (for they are no more than that) remained undiscovered in Oriental art for the very good reason that they were not found necessary? Oriental art has its own methods of representing space, and perhaps its own emotional attitude to space. Every form of art, according to Riegl, is the expression of a will, the fulfilment of a desire. Oriental art satisfied the Oriental artist because it 'realized' a certain conception of reality. He sought rhythm in his line, harmony in his colour, and precision in his form, and he found these qualities without recourse to perspective and chiaroscuro. In the end he had a work of art which fulfilled one of the primary functions of a work of art, which is to objectify our sense of visual pleasure, simply to please the sight. But the Oriental artist knew that the means he employed to this end (rhythm, harmony, precision) also served a certain symbolic function: to represent the eternal order and harmony of the universe. But these metaphysical values are read into the work of art by the spectator—they are not a conscious aim of the artist during the process of creation.

[50]

THE SIGNIFICANCE OF CÉZANNE

'I have not tried to reproduce nature: I have represented it'. The saying is Cézanne's, but there is some equivocation in the word 'nature'. Cézanne was certainly thinking of the appearance of things visible to the eye: their objective existence. His desire was to 'represent' the things in themselves as present in his sensibility: to get away from the exact mechanical reproduction of that imaginary mirror-like level on to which, in the act of vision, we conventionally project things. To get away, too, from the desires extraneous to the one aim of rendering the sensation—away from the ideas, passions or beliefs which so often inspired the painters in the past. It was, in a sense, a metaphysical conception of painting: a notion that there existed in the sense-data of the painter, a 'real' vision independent of the intellect and beyond, at the back of, the sensations: a raw material underlying appearances. If the artist could render this, he would be able to represent reality in its original structure and force, the objective reality from which proceed all consequential emotions and ideas.

This conception of art has something in common with the Oriental conception, but is more objective. The Eastern painter's sense of rhythm and harmony was intuitive rather than perceptual —his ideal was to become identified with the organic processes of nature and to create his work of art in the same spirit. The difference between a Sung landscape painting and a Cézanne landscape is the difference between a synthetic and an analytic approach to the subject. Cézanne's intention goes beyond the theory of symbolism as formulated by Sérusier; beyond any aim or achievement of Gauguin. But Cézanne was a simple man, though a passionate one; and he had no Sérusier to formulate a system on the basis of his passionate practice, his dogged insight. His method was, in a sense, still empirical. He kept to his ideal of the 'real' vision, but he sought

[51]

to arrive at the representation of this vision by tentative means. He explored the structure and the colours of an object, tirelessly, endlessly, with maddening persistence, until he felt satisfied that the forms and colours on his canvas did in fact represent his 'real' vision. It was a method that required the patience of a saint, and because saints are very rare (even among artists) it was not a method likely to become popular. I would go farther and say that it is not necessarily the most appropriate method: it is possible to maintain that vision is essentially instantaneous and must be represented by some method which matches this instantaneity of vision with a spontaneity of expression.

Such a method was first consciously practised by Henri Matisse and it remains one of the most characteristic in contemporary art: it is the first of the three theories which dominate the contemporary scene, and into which I think the complexity of modern art can be resolved.

THE METHOD OF HENRI MATISSE

Jacques Emile Blanche, in his survey of the plastic arts from 1870 to the present day, published in 1931,[1] gives an interesting account of Matisse in action:

'The only time that Matisse revealed to me his usual practice or method', he writes, 'he told me that when he is in the South he sets out with his tackle immediately after breakfast. He looks for a subject, sets up his easel. At mid-day, either he has finished his sketch, and signs it; or considering it spoilt, he decides to do another the next day. It is the extravagance of a dandy who throws to the wash first one white tie, then another, if he has crumpled them in knotting, and will go on using up ties until his skill has triumphed. The "fait du premier coup", the hit-or-miss method of Matisse is at the other extreme of Cézanne's slowness.'

[1] Op. cit.

To this we might add an explanation given by Matisse himself, which I have already quoted in *The Meaning of Art* (3rd edn. (1951), §86):

'Expression for me is not to be found in the passion which blazes from a face or which is made evident by some violent gesture. It is in the whole disposition of my picture—the place occupied by the figures, the empty space around them, the proportions—everything plays its part. Composition is the art of arranging in a decorative manner the various elements which the painter uses to express his sentiments. In a picture every separate part will be visible and will take up that position, principal or secondary, which suits it best. Everything which has no utility in the picture is for that reason harmful. A work of art implies a harmony of everything together (une harmonie d'ensemble): every superfluous detail will occupy, in the mind of the spectator, the place of some other detail which is essential.'

That was written a long time ago, in 1908, and in view of the charges which have been levelled against Matisse's work, even by friendly critics, I doubt if later he would have emphasized so strongly the decorative function of a painting. For the general tendency of his critics has been to admit the charm of colour, the vividness, the fascination, the miraculous technique of Matisse's compositions; and then to qualify this praise by saying: But it is only decorative: it is deceptive, heady, sensuous, attractive like a good poster, but no more. Even his portraits, these critics say, are still bouquets of flowers, patterns of ribbons and silks, expressing a fine taste and effectively (that is to say, grotesquely) arranged on a sketchy framework. An alluring feast for the senses—but spirituality, humanity, criticism of life, verisimilitude—none of these great and comprehensible qualities which have distinguished the art of the past—even the art of a Cézanne—is present in the art of Matisse.

We touch here on fundamental problems of aesthetics. The

[53]

theorist of modern art, in defence of Matisse, must claim that no definition of painting which does not include in some way the concept of *form* can survive application for long. This is probably true of all branches of art, even of literature, where content might seem to have so much relevance as to be inseparable from form. In a sense, of course, it is inseparable, because form is something *given*, an endowment, and always implies a recipient, a thing formed. But the thing formed—and this is the clue to the whole of the modern development of art—can be subjective as well as objective —can be the spontaneous product of the emergent sensibility of the artist.[1] I would like to continue the literary parallel for a little longer, and quote a passage from a great critical work published as long ago as 1870—De Sanctis's *History of Italian Literature*. He is speaking of Dante's first conceptions of his *Divine Comedy*, and says:

'The early time of a poet's inspiration—that tentative time which is so highly dramatic—is hidden to criticism. It is the time of silent contest of the poet with himself, of vague outlines, of coming and going in his mind; it is the intimate history of the poet. When a subject comes into the brain of a creative writer, it at once dissolves that part of reality which suggested it. The earthly images seem to fluctuate, like objects in a mass of vapour seen from above. The figures—the trees, the towers, the houses—disintegrate, become fragmentary. To create reality, a poet must first have the force to kill it. But instantly the fragments draw together again, in love with each other, seeking one another, coming together with desire, with the obscure presentiment of the new life to which they are destined. And the first real moment of creation in that tumultuous and fragmentary world is the moment when those fragments find a point, a centre around which they can press. It is then that the poet's creation comes out from the unlimited, which makes it fluctuant, and takes on a definite form—it is then that it comes to birth. It is born

[1] See note, p. 97 below.

[54]

and lives, or rather it develops gradually, in conformity with its essence.'[1]

I find this description of the poetic process of quite exact application to the painting of Matisse, and generally I believe that the aesthetics of form, propounded by De Sanctis in relation to literature and generalized in our own time for all the arts by Benedetto Croce, sanctions, to an extent not realized by the Neapolitan philosopher himself, the tendencies of modern art. But dispensing with Croce, we may apply De Sanctis's analysis of the poetic process to the plastic process as represented by Matisse. Perhaps I might first quote, as adding still further to the detailed description of the actual process, some few sentences from another French critic of art, M. Claude Roger-Marx:[2]

'His canvases, whilst having the appearance of a first state or a rough sketch, seem quite definitive to the mind of their painter; though done rapidly, they were conceived slowly. To understand them, one should have heard the artist, with perfect sincerity, explaining his intentions. Then, all which one had thought the result of chance appears contrived. Where the public find only provocation and incoherence, he has only sought style at whatever cost. Not one of all these distortions that cannot be justified. This lack of expression in the literary sense, plastically speaking is expression itself. These apparent abstractions have only one end in view: to express the sentiment, which we might almost call religious, that the artist has of life. These disfigured figures—these tortured bodies, dream only of an act of equilibrium, something analogous to a good armchair in which one relaxes.'

Except when he speaks vaguely of a religious sentiment of life, this critic does not give us any clue to the essence, the point around which, to revert to De Sanctis's description, the sensations of the

---

[1] *History of Italian Literature* by Francesco De Sanctis. Trans. by Joan Redfern. (Oxford Univ. Press, 1932.)
[2] Quoted by J. E. Blanche, *op. cit.* p. 253.

artist recompose themselves. In Dante's case it was the moral idea. In Matisse's case I think we might describe it as *integral vision*.[1]

THE THEORY OF INTEGRAL VISION

The development of art in any civilization can be related to the development of vision.[2] In a micro-cosmic way, we can see the same development in a child's drawings. The representation of extension, of direction, of depth, are slowly and painfully acquired in primitive societies because until the artist has learned to analyse his power of vision, he is ignorant, not only of *how* he sees, but of *what* he sees. Just as we now infer the roundness of the earth, so at one period the artist (in the manner of the child) had to infer the extension of plane surfaces, the different directions of the branches of a tree, the placing of all objects in a space continuum. Art evolved as the analysis of vision. We have become so used to this analytical vision, that we hardly realize that vision is in fact primarily *integral*. Now in one sentence, the aim of Matisse is to restore the integral vision.

Take any field of vision—a landscape, the scene before you now, if you lift your eyes. To get a complete view of the scene, your vision must shift about from point to point. When it has, so to speak, roamed over the whole field, then by an act of synthesis the mind retains the scene as a whole. Unconsciously, as a general rule, we focus on a central point, or prominent light, and the rest of the scene arranges itself rather vaguely round this point. Some things we only see out of the corner of the eye. If a rival highlight or prominent object enters the field of vision, then we are in doubt which to focus on, and suffer from a sense of visual discomfort. Visual comfort is a kind of equilibrium, or, to use the words of the critic I

[1] A phrase I owe to the late Matthew Prichard, to whose conversations on aesthetics I was at one time greatly indebted.
[2] Cf. G. Britsch: *Theorie der bildenden Kunst.* 2nd edn. Munich, 1930.

quoted a few minutes ago (actually, Matisse's own words), something analogous to a good armchair in which one relaxes.

Beauty, to use the good mediaeval definition, is *id quod visum placet*, that which being seen pleases. And in a very real sense, plastic form and linear rhythm resolve into questions of visual comfort. The rhythm of a composition may have other qualities: it may be static and restful, or dynamic and exciting. But primarily form in plastic art is related to a pleasant sense of visual comfort.

Matisse seizes on this physiological platitude and makes it a principle of composition—not, as former painters have in general done, by reconstructing the analytical mental process by means of which we construct a field of vision, but by holding on to a fixed focus, a single line of sight, and painting passionately, intensely, swiftly what the eye in this immediate act perceives.

It follows that the results of such a method of painting must be viewed with the same immediate vision. In looking at a picture by Matisse, we must fix our gaze on a central point, hold that focus, and the rest of the picture, which to the analytical vision seems meaninglessly distorted, now falls into position, acquires its meaning and its due relationship. It is one more principle of unity added to those which have governed the historical tradition of European painting—the subjective or emotional unity of the Italian and the Flemish primitives, the architectonic unity of the Classical Renaissance and of Cézanne, the dynamic unity of the Baroque period. Now it is the unity of a focal vision, and that implies an integration of so many of the principles which have hitherto been separately striven for—it implies balance or symmetry, and certainly an architectonic structure. The elements of the picture must be so arranged that the eye holds its focus with ease.

The part played by colour in this synthesis is of the utmost importance, but in this respect Matisse does not represent any distinctively modern development. Colours were never so pure, so positive, nor so plangent, and no doubt in this respect Matisse has introduced into modern art qualities of colour harmony derived from such remote sources as Persian miniature painting and mediaeval stained glass. This plenitude of colour is the final expression of the certainty of his creative instinct.

Matisse's paintings have been compared, not unreasonably, with children's drawings. Because in both you have the same pre-logical vision, the same delight of the innocent eye.

Chapter III

EXPRESSIONISM
THE THEORY OF SUBJECTIVE INTEGRITY

Before describing those types of modern art that betray in greater or lesser degree the absence of any desire to reproduce the phenomenal world, there is a whole division of modern art which, whilst it has some of the subjective and symbolist qualities of the types of art just discussed, remains linked, if not to the innocent, at least to the observant eye. We might characterize this type by saying that it depends for its subjective appeal, not so much on formal elements, as on the emotional content of the objects or events represented. It is frankly a 'literary' art, but a good deal of the art of the past (the art of the Van Eycks and of Rembrandt, for example) is just such a literary art; and in any case, as Gauguin said, what does it matter so long as it is art? We must therefore give it a place in our survey, in defiance of those critics who are too exclusively wedded to the purist or intellectual prejudices of the Paris school.

VISUAL v. POETIC UNITY

There is, of course, a considerable problem involved here. It is not merely the difference between an emphasis on form and an emphasis on content: there is rather a direct opposition between two different principles of unity in the painting—what Roger Fry has called the principles of visual and of poetic unity. In an Introduction he wrote to an edition of the *Discourses* of Sir Joshua Reynolds, published in 1905, Roger Fry makes a very illuminating

[59]

comparison between typical pictures by Van Eyck and Rubens. After describing the completeness and unity of the formal pattern in Rubens's painting, he turns to the Van Eyck (it is the famous altarpiece at Ghent) and points out that in all its mass of detail we can find no large pattern, no dominating silhouette, none of the leading lines and large contrasts which bind together Rubens's design: there is no system of subordination by which the eye can deal with a whole group as a single mass, and count it as a single unit in the design. 'And yet,' he goes on to admit, 'though there is no unity in Reynolds's sense, if we examine the picture in detail we shall find the most marvellous sense of relationship in the parts— not a face of all these hundreds but has that stamp of uniformity which makes for us a definite character, not a fold of drapery that does not fall harmoniously with its neighbours, not a spray of foliage which fails of the rhythm expressive of organic life. As the eye follows along any contour it will be conscious of purpose, and singular rightness of purpose, in each minutest change of form; it will find that down to the smallest atomic divisions of the parts the pervading sense of creative purpose informs and animates the design. Now, this implies a highly developed sense of relationship and rhythm, and these are the essentials of that unity which Reynolds so rightly praises. What are we to say, then, of Van Eyck's failure to attain the same visible unity in his whole composition which the separate parts discover so unmistakably? The answer is that his parts cohere by reason of a different principle. Visibly, indeed, they cohere only by the general symmetry of disposition, which is here a weak and negative force, affording, as it were, an intellectual approval of order rather than any strong visual gratification or assistance. But we must consider that the unity is here essentially poetic and imaginative, and not visual.'

That type of modern art which I have in mind is exactly described by such words, though, naturally, we must extend our notion of what constitutes a 'poetic idea'. Even the Flemish School was not bound to the 'miraculous beauties' with which the Van Eycks filled their picture; the sombre mysticism of Van der Goes, the grimness of Hieronymus Bosch, the realism of Breughel, are all justified by the same principle of emotional unity; whereas in the German School a masterpiece like Grünewald's Isenheim altarpiece triumphs over the most gruesome ugliness by virtue of this very principle.

THE SIGNIFICANCE OF EDVARD MUNCH

The beginnings of the modern German school, which stands in such isolation and distinction from the Paris school, are to be sought in the art of the Scandinavian, Edvard Munch. Munch is an artist whose work is still little known in this country, but there is no doubt that he has been one of the most important influences of the last fifty years. He occupies, in relation to the modern German movement, a position comparable to Cézanne's in French painting. We might say that he saved German art from a slavish following of the Post-Impressionist school; he returned to a mode of expression more consonant with the nordic genius.

Munch was born in Norway in 1863. He first studies at Oslo under Christian Krogh, the greatest representative of the Impressionist movement in Norway. From 1889 to 1892, and again from 1895 to 1897, he was in Paris, but Paris had little to teach him, or little that he cared to absorb. His characteristic individuality is already seen in the pictures he painted before he went to Paris. Between his visits to Paris, and from 1897 to 1909, Munch lived mostly in Germany, and there he felt free to develop in a sympathetic atmosphere. That sympathetic atmosphere soon crystallized into a group, known as 'Die Brücke' (the Bridge) which acknowledged Munch as their master, and from this group originated that much wider movement in modern German art known as Expressionism—a movement entirely distinct from the contemporary

French movement,[1] but one which ought to be sympathetic to our own Northern temperament.

Munch's early work shows a preoccupation with dramatic values; titles like 'The Sick Child' and 'The Dead Mother' sufficiently indicate its general character. In his early years Munch must have felt the extraordinary superficiality of French Impressionism, occupied, to the exclusion of all other interests, with problems of light and colour, texture and composition. Such problems had their interest for Munch too; but beyond them was the greater problem of human life, and this he found far from inconsistent with aesthetic expression.

This emphasis on emotional unity in art, on the element of human feeling, was *one* influence which Munch passed on to German Expressionism. There was also a technical influence. The early pictures of Munch are already painted in a bold vigorous manner; the vitality of the brush strokes is not lost in a general smoothness. As Munch's art develops, this quality grows more emphatic. Roughly speaking, there are two alternative methods in painting— the method of tone and the method of line. If you desire depth and plastic cohesion in your picture, then you must develop your tonal relations at the expense of linear outline: but if, on the other hand, you desire movement and rhythm, then you must develop linear emphasis at the expense of tone. Munch was in something of a dilemma, because tone, so readily expressive of spiritual values, is dear to the northern artist; but so also is vitality, and vitality is best expressed by movement. On the whole we may say that Munch has sacrificed tone to line, and in this the modern German movement has to a great extent followed him. But there has been an attempt, which can be traced in the works of Munch, to obviate the limitations of the linear or graphic method, and to make it, in spite of everything, expressive of spiritual or psychological values. This

[1] Rouault is an exception, and in Belgium there is a vigorous expressionist school including such painters as Permeke, Tygat and Van den Berghe.

has been done by developing a quality which might be called monumentality, a quality which the best German Impressionists, such as Liebermann and Corinth, share with Munch. Lines enclose planes, and these planes, in terms of paint, are so definite in form and so intense in colour, and so firmly organized in a structural sense, that they take on the depth and atmosphere of solid things.

THE BRÜCKE GROUP

The group known as the Brücke, largely inspired by the art of Munch, was founded by three art students at Dresden in 1905. The eldest of them, Ernst Ludwig Kirchner, then a young man of 25, was trained as an architect; he was the most energetic and forceful member of the group. His two companions, Erich Heckel and Karl Schmidt-Rottluff, were three or four years younger. Kirchner found his first inspiration in African and Polynesian savage art, which he saw in the Dresden Ethnological Museum; and this exotic influence, which has been so powerful in modern art in France as well as in Germany, first found its real impetus in the Brücke group. The other influence which strongly affected this group was Van Gogh, and Van Gogh has had far more influence in Germany than in France; and this is only natural, for in all his characteristics Van Gogh is primarily a Northern artist—Teutonic not Latin, Gothic not Classic: he is an influence which the German artist can absorb without being in any way false to his native tradition. The art of primitive races, the art of Van Gogh, and then the art of Munch—these are the three influences which formed the first of the distinctively German schools in modern art.[1]

[1] The period of intensive action lasted from 1904 to 1909. By then these artists had formed their personal styles—had found themselves, as we say. In 1906 Max Pechstein, born in 1881, and Emil Nolde, a much older artist—he was born in 1867—joined the group. Much later, in 1910, Otto Müller, an artist from Silesia who was born in 1874 and died in 1930, was also admitted. Three years later, in 1913, the Brücke collapsed: it had served its purpose.

The general characteristics of the group might be deduced from the influences which went to its formation: the bold brushwork of Van Gogh and Munch, the decorative use of colour typical of these masters, the barbaric splendour of savage art. To these add, perhaps, a certain Germanic brutality which needed no encouragement; and at the same time a tendency towards transcendentalism and psychological content common to the native German tradition.

EMIL NOLDE: NORDIC SENSIBILITY

The work of Emil Nolde is too individual to be included within a general description of the Brücke group. Nolde is one of the most important of modern German artists, a vigorous draughtsman, powerful in design, supreme in colour. In his autobiography he defines his attitude to art in a few sentences that are significant for the German school in general. 'The art of an artist', he writes, 'must be his own art. It is, I believe, in externals always a continuous chain of little inventions, little technical discoveries of one's own, in one's relation to the tool, the material and the colours. What the artist learns matters little. What he himself discovers has a real worth for him, and gives him the necessary incitement to work. When such creative activity ceases, when there are no more difficulties or problems, external or internal, to solve, then the fire is quickly extinguished. . . . An ability to learn was never a sign of genius.'

What is so significant in Nolde's autobiography is the definite reaction he shows to French art. Already in 1898 he is thanking God that he has never been attracted by the French style, that he has not been caught in the net of any Parisian Circe. For Manet's 'bright beauty' and for Daumier's 'dramatic greatness' he felt an exceptional sympathy; but Renoir, Monet, Pissarro were too 'sweet' for his bitter northern sense. In 1900 he went to Paris, studied at Julian's, met artists of many countries. But of this experience he

[64]

writes: 'Paris had given me so little, and yet I had hoped for so much.' He returned to Germany, to listen to his own inner voice, to follow his own instinct. Then came the Brücke, to which, however, he gave allegiance for only two years. In 1913 he made a journey to the South Seas—to Java and Burma—and that experience undoubtedly affected his later development, in much the same way that a similar experience affected Gauguin. It intensified his colour sensibility; it gave him the sense of exotic magic. This man whose very being was nurtured on Northern mists and twilight fantasy, found the fulfilment of his yearnings in the full light and barbaric splendour of the tropics. It has been said that in all great artists extremes meet. These extremes meet in Nolde. For he does not succumb to barbaric magic, he is not overwhelmed by it. He takes it and turns it to his own uses. He makes it express his own Northern consciousness, as it was never expressed since the Gothic period (which also, remember, is a compound of extremes, of Eastern exoticism and Northern spirituality). That is why Nolde takes us back to the Middle Ages for a parallel—to the stained-glass windows of Augsburg and Strasburg, to the coloured wood blocks and illuminated manuscripts of seven or eight centuries ago.

EXPRESSIONISM

Near to the Brücke may be placed those artists associated with a spiritual tradition common to all the contemporary arts in Germany. This is not a group in the conscious, organized sense. It consists of three or four artists who have in common a certain relentless realism—even a cynicism—which is partly a social protest, but a protest intensified by the experience of war. The artists I am referring to—Max Beckmann, Otto Dix, George Grosz—were all born round about 1890. They have all painted war pictures of a grimness unequalled by anything in other countries. The phrase

Die neue Sachlichkeit, 'The New Objectivity', was coined to describe them, and the coiner of the phrase, Dr Hartlaub, the Director of the Mannheim Art Gallery, has explained it in the following way: 'The expression ought really to apply as a label to that type of modern realism which bears a socialistic flavour. It was related to the general contemporary feeling in Germany of resignation and cynicism after a period of exuberant hopes (which had found an outlet in Expressionism). Cynicism and resignation are the negative side of the Neue Sachlichkeit; the positive side expresses itself in enthusiasm for immediate reality—the result of a desire to take things entirely objectively on a material basis without immediately investing them with ideal implications.'[1] That explanation makes the tendency of this group quite clear. Such realism, sardonic in its essence, is not likely to be acceptable to those who want art to be pretty, or even to be beautiful in the classic sense. It is no lovelier than the sardonic humour of Swift; or of Rowlandson. George Grosz, indeed, by attacking the most deeply seated hypocrisies of our social life, our habitual sensualities, can only be accepted in a mood of spiritual asceticism, though everywhere his sensitive technique has its fine surgical beauty.

Though 'Die neue Sachlichkeit' is no longer a battlecry, and though Expressionism in general was for a time political heresy in Germany, it has far too strong an appeal to the nordic temperament—and far too obvious analogies in the historical art of Northern Europe—to be dismissed as a transitory phase of modern art. Its values are not aesthetically 'pure'; nor are the values of Van Eyck, Breughel, Rembrandt and many other Northern artists who use the technique of painting, not so much with the intention of creating an object of beauty, but rather as a mean of communicating the emotions which they feel with overpowering intensity. For there are at least these two modes of art: the mode

---

[1] Quoted by Alfred H. Barr, Jr., *German Painting and Sculpture*. New York, 1931.

[66]

of intellectual vision, whose end is absolute beauty; and the mode
of emotional expression, whose end is the communication of sympathetic feeling—the mode of Rubens (but much more typically
the mode of Raphael and the Italian masters generally) and the
mode of Van Eyck—to-day the mode of Picasso or Braque and the
mode of Nolde or Rouault. Even that completely insurrectionary
movement known in France as Surréalisme, whose general characteristics are described on a later page, fits into this division: it is
a mode of emotional expressionism, even when its end must be
described as the communication of antipathetic rather than sympathetic feeling.

Further developments of a specifically Nordic sensibility took
coherent shape when the Blaue Reiter group was formed in Munich
in 1911. In so far as this group had a separate philosophy of art, it
owed it largely to Wassily Kandinsky (1866–1944), a Russian by
birth. Kandinsky's treatise on *The Spiritual in Art*,[1] of which I shall
give some account in Chapter VI, is one of the earliest and remains
one of the most comprehensive approaches to the subject of expressionism. While writing his book Kandinsky discovered abstraction
—that is to say, he found (almost accidentally, if we are to believe
his own statements), that the 'internal necessity' which he desired
to express could be most adequately represented by a precisely determined non-figurative symbol. From 1910 onwards he experi-
mented with what might be described as a calligraphic system of
notation which is distinct from the figurative expressionism of the
Brücke group. Other members of the Blaue Reiter group—Franz
Marc and August Macke in particular—though far more eclectic
than the artist of the Brücke group, may still be described as Expressionists, but the development of these two artists was brought
to an untimely end, for they were both killed in the war.

[1] *Über das Geistige in der Kunst*, Munich, 1912. Trans. London (*The Art of Spiritual Harmony*) 1914, and New York (*On the Spiritual in Art*), 1947.

[67]

A contemporary philosopher, Hannah Arendt, in a pregnant footnote,[1] has called attention to the basic fallacy of the expressionist theory of art. The artist, she contends, whether painter or sculptor or poet or musician, produces 'worldly' objects, objects of use and of commerce, and no one calls upon him to 'express himself'. The process of reification, the artist's ability to give material existence to his perceptions, has nothing in common with 'the highly questionable and, at any rate, wholly unartistic practice of expressionism. Expressionist art, but not abstract art, is a contradiction in terms'. This is true, in so far as the artist insists on expressionism as such, on self-expression as a justification for his activity; but in practice many of the expressionists surpassed this aim, and in spite of their 'selves' succeeded in creating worldly objects of universal value.

[1] *The Human Condition* (Chicago, 1958), p. 323n.

Chapter IV

TOWARDS ABSTRACTION
THE THEORY OF PURE FORM

That disregard for the synthetic powers of the mind, that desire to return to the integral vision, the prelogical state of perception which characterizes the art of Matisse, is, of course, a step towards subjectivism in art. But the act of painting is far from being wholly subjective, even in this direct method, for the activity of the painter is still related to an object, even although that object is the focus of a field of vision rather than a three-dimensional survey of that field. Indeed, it is possible to hold that the method of Matisse is the truly objective one, and that any other method, relying as it does on a mental or intellectual construction designed to show the relation of all the objects in a field of vision, is infinitely more subjective. Dr Thouless once carried out some interesting experiments at Glasgow University which show that there is a considerable divergence between what the eye actually sees, and a perspective representation of the same object. The importance of this discovery justifies lengthy quotations from the journal in which it was first published.[1]

'Experiments were performed on the shapes of objects viewed obliquely, the apparent brightness of differently illuminated surfaces of different reflectivity, the apparent sizes of objects at different distances, and the apparent convergence of parallel lines receding from the observer. In all of these cases it was found that what was seen was intermediate between what was given in peripheral

[1] 'Phenomenal Regression to the Real Object', *British Journal of Psy-chology*, vol. xxi, pt 4; vol. xxii, pts 1 and 3 (1931–2).

stimulation and the "real" character of the object. To this effect of
the character of the "real" object of the phenomenal character we
may give the name "phenomenal regression to the real object".'
(Vol. xxi, p. 358.)

'The Child learning to draw in accordance with the laws of perspective is being taught to draw a projection of the object he is
looking at on the plane of the picture. In order to discover what are
the shapes, sizes, etc., he is required to draw, he is taught to use
the device of holding his pencil at arm's length and, with one eye
closed, to make measurements along it. . . .

'That the laws of perspective do correctly describe the ways in
which shapes, sizes, relationships of lines, etc., must appear on such
a plane projection cannot, of course, be denied, and it is obvious
that the experiments on phenomenal regression have no bearing on
this question. Nor do they throw any doubt on the usefulness of the
above devices for determining the characters of the plane projection.

'Teachers of perspective are, however, often not content to make
these legitimate claims for the laws of perspective. They are inclined to say that the laws of perspective are the laws of the ways in
which we "see", and to suggest that the above-mentioned methods
of measurement with ruler, etc., are devices for finding out how we
"really" see things. . . .

'Some artists . . . have departed very far from perspective drawing. I have found that certain of the post-impressionist painters
drew inclined objects in ratios which were about those of the phenomenal shapes as measured in the . . . experiments. It seems prob-
able, therefore, that these were actually drawing the phenomenal
and not the perspective figure. . . .

'Experiment shows that the extent of phenomenal regression
differs very greatly from one individual to another. It follows,
therefore, that a drawing which would look right to one person
might look very wrong to another. It is possible that those artists

[70]

whose departures from perspective seem to most observers to produce distortion of shape are simply those with abnormally large
indices of regression.' (Vol. xxii, pp. 27–29.)

THE INNOCENT AND THE
INSTRUCTED EYE

Scientific perspective is thus a construction of the intellect, and
not a direct perception. The rounded ellipse which we see in
Cézanne's painting of a *compotier* may be actually nearer to the
ellipse seen by the uninstructed eye than would be the ellipse
which we painfully teach the mind of the child to construct according to *a priori* principles.

If now we may generalize, we can say that if an artist has arrived
at the stage of realizing, (1) that a representation of the 'real' character of an object is an intellectual or 'objective' construction, and
(2) that the phenomenal figure which is the only direct experience
of the eye is a 'subjective' experience; then it is natural for such an
artist to desire to make a further step. But he will realize that this
further step can be in two divergent directions. In one direction,
he can affirm the intellectual or objective nature of his activity, but
instead of pretending to reproduce by this means the 'real' character of an object, the visible scene, he can proceed on other *a priori*
principles. Regarding the object merely as a point of departure, a
stimulus, he can create a number of variations, exactly as the
musician takes a simple theme as a point of departure, and, by
observing certain laws, projects a composition sanctioned by its
consistent form. That is one direction in which our hypothetical
artist can develop. In the other direction, he can affirm the subjective nature of his activity, and abandoning all attempts to reproduce even the phenomenal character of an object, or indeed any
forms given by the direct experience of the eye, he can proceed to
project on to his canvas an arrangement of lines and colours which

are entirely subjective in origin, and which, if they obey any laws at all, obey the laws of their own origination. Each work of art is then a law unto itself. These are, in fact, the two theories which I think will cover all the remaining manifestations of modern art.

The first I will call *the theory of abstraction*; the second, *the theory of automatism.*

PLATO'S ANTICIPATION OF
THE THEORY OF ABSTRACTION

The first theory, as has already been noted by various writers, has relations with the classical theory of form, and some of the apologists of *Cubism*, which is the name given to the first of the modern manifestations of abstract art, have not hesitated to claim the label of neo-classicism. The best classical expression of the theory of abstract art is found in Plato. I would like to quote a significant passage from the *Philebus* (51 B); Socrates and Protarchus are the speakers:

'*S*. True pleasures are those which arise from the colours we call beautiful and from shapes; and most of the pleasures of smell and sound. True pleasures arise from all those things the want of which is not felt as painful but the satisfaction from which is consciously pleasant and unconditioned by pain.'

'*P*. But again, Socrates, what do we mean by these?'

'*S*. Certainly what I mean is not quite clear, but I must try to make it so. I do not now intend by beauty of shapes what most people would expect, such as that of living creatures or pictures, but, for the purpose of my argument, I mean straight lines and curves and the surfaces or solid forms produced out of these by lathes and rulers and squares, if you understand me. For I mean that these things are not beautiful relatively, like other things, but always and naturally and absolutely; and they have their proper

[72]

PLATO'S ANTICIPATION OF THE THEORY OF ABSTRACTION

pleasures, no way depending on the itch of desire. And I mean colours of the same kind, with the same kind of beauty and pleasures. Is that clear or not?'

'*P*. I am doing my best, Socrates, but do your best to make it clearer.'

'*S*. Well, I mean that such sounds as are pure and smooth and yield a single pure tone are not beautiful relatively to anything else but in their own proper nature, and produce their proper pleasures.'[1]

The *Philebus* is Plato's last work, and here we have a definite abandonment of the unfortunate theory of *mimesis*, or art conceived as a technique for the direct imitation of the appearance of things; and moreover we are no longer committed to the theory, inherent in Greek philosophy since Pythagoras, which identifies art with beauty, and explains it in terms of harmonic proportion. This latter theory was to be given final expression by Aristotle (for example, he says: The essential characters composing beauty are order, symmetry, and definiteness) and from Aristotle it passed into scholastic philosophy. 'For beauty there are three requirements,' writes St Thomas Aquinas. 'First, a certain wholeness or perfection, for whatever is incomplete is, so far, ugly; second, a due proportion or harmony; and third, clarity, so that brightly coloured things are called beautiful.' And this theory was taken over by the classicizing tendencies of the Renaissance, and, indeed, gets its perfect expression in the art of the sixteenth century. But this is not the theory of beauty put forward by Plato in the *Philebus*; Plato does not commit himself to anything so definite, to anything so mathematical and rational. He says: 'I do not now intend by beauty of shapes what most people would expect, such as that of living creatures or pictures.' In that sentence he rejects the mimetic theory of beauty. 'I mean', he goes on to say, 'straight lines and

[1] Trans. by E. F. Carritt: *Philosophies of Beauty* (Oxford, 1931), pp. 29–30.

[73]

curves and the surfaces or solid forms produced out of these by lathes and rulers and squares.' And these things, he says, are not beautiful relatively, like other things (that is to say, they do not depend for their beauty on their use, or purpose, or relation one to another) but are beautiful always and naturally and absolutely.

CÉZANNE'S APPROACH TO THE THEORY

It might be possible to trace the vicissitudes of this idea through the centuries, but for my present purpose it will be better to leap from Plato to Cézanne. Cézanne was not, of course, a philosopher, or only a natural one, and as in the case of Gauguin, but at a later date, it has been left to others to formulate the theories implicit in Cézanne's work. But it is important to realize first of all that Cézanne foreshadowed a definite break, not merely with the academic notion of painting which prevailed everywhere during the nineteenth century, but also with what was in his day the revolutionary school of Impressionism. The unfortunate word 'Post-impressionism' was invented, and it is unfortunate because it leads the innocent to suppose that Post-impressionism was a development of Impressionism. But that is far from the truth. When Cézanne, in *his* innocent way, said that his aim was 'to do Poussin again after nature', and 'to make out of impressionism something as solid and enduring as the art of the museums', he was definitely renouncing the aim of that tradition which began with Constable and ended with Manet. *Their* art had staked everything on the impression of natural vitality conveyed by the work of art; Cézanne staked everything on the revelation of the inherent form. He did not want to adopt the *a priori* notions of form which the Renaissance had inherited from Aristotelian philosophy; such notions of form were imposed on art from without. Cézanne sought his form in the object itself, and he strove, with all the passion and integrity of genius, to reveal the structure latent in satisfying natural sub-

[74]

jects. This involved an emphasis on planes, volumes, and outlines which tended to give his paintings a geometrical organization; and Cézanne himself said that nature could be resolved into the cylinder, the sphere and the cone. Which is very near Plato's 'surfaces and solid forms'.

I must, however, admit this qualification in respect of Cézanne. He did not conceive his volumes in outline, geometrically, but in contrasted colours; and that is really the individual distinction of Cézanne: a sensibility to form expressed in colour. 'To paint,' he said, 'was to register his colour sensations.' Everything else—all values of atmosphere and perspective—is sacrificed to this end, sacrificed to the organization of his colour sensations. 'When colour has its richness, form has its plenitude' is another of his rare revealing aphorisms. This conception of form built up in colour, a colour synthesis, is perhaps a difficult one to realize, especially for people who are weak in colour sensibility: it is, however, the essential quality of Cézanne's art. In a sense, it brings him nearer to St Thomas's definition than to Plato's; for St Thomas, as we have seen, insisted on a clarity of bright colours as one of the essentials of beauty.

GEOMETRIC TYPES OF ART

Before going on to describe the theory of abstraction developed on the basis of Cézanne's practice, it is necessary to refer to one other type of art of which there are several historical examples. It is often confused with abstraction, and certainly modern developments in abstract art owe as much to it as to Cézanne. I refer to what is generally known as 'geometricizing' or 'stylized' art: a type found in the early period of Greek art, in Byzantine, Scandinavian and early Gothic art, and in various kinds of savage art. The essence of this kind of art, as distinct from the art of Cézanne, is that it is in no sense organic. It is difficult to generalize about a phenomenon so widely spread in time and origins; but essentially it is a distortion in the representation of a natural object in the interests of rhythm. It is generally confined to the representation of single objects—a god, an animal, or a plant, and if applied to larger patterns, then becomes a rigidly symmetrical design: the organization, that is to say, if any, is of a proportionate, harmonic type. But the essential character of this style is seen in a single object, for example, a Scythian gold ornament in the so-called Animal Style, and that character may be defined as an emphasis of the rhythmical content of natural forms to the greatest extent consistent with a recognition of the object represented. But in the degenerate types of this art the original object is lost and we get instead a formal symmetrical pattern of no great aesthetic significance.

The interest in formal structure evoked by Cézanne's method coincided with a renewed interest in geometric types of art—particularly Byzantine art and tribal art: perhaps, to some extent, the two interests fed one another. But the final result of these interests in the sphere of art, was the contemporary Cubist school.

CUBISM

This is a fairly limited school, but a very consistent, and a very persistent one. In France it originally consisted of artists like Gris, Braque, Ozenfant, Jeanneret, Delaunay, Marcoussis, Metzinger, Gleizes and Léger; in Germany, Marc, Feininger and Baumeister. In France Picasso for a time exerted the preponderant influence; whilst in Germany Kandinsky, with his writings as well as his paintings, took the lead. Both Matisse and Derain once painted in this style.

The Cubists proper, although they display considerable variations of manner and even of method, nevertheless illustrate a coherent theory of art, and I believe that this theory is *nearly* the same theory as that expressed by Plato in the passage from the

[76]

Philebus which I have quoted. Cézanne was, as I hope I have made
clear, still bound to a theory of equivalence: he believed that in
some way his painting did represent the nature of an object; or, at any
rate, represented the sensation given by the nature of the object.
His art, in spite of its organization, was still a mimetic art. But the
cubist, taking the object as a point of departure, abstracts from it, to
revert to the words of Plato, by means of lathes, rulers and squares,
the inherent straight lines and curves, surfaces and solid forms.[1]
    Described in so many words, this process of abstraction might
have the appearance of a mechanical process, leaving little room for
the play of the artist's individual sensibility. Actually, nothing
could be more distinct than the personality, the individuality, of
the work of the various cubist painters I have mentioned. No one
would ever confuse a work by Braque with a work by Léger. Far
from emptying a work of the artist's personality, this process of
abstraction, by removing the sentimental mask of actuality, leaves
that personality free to shine out clearly. Landscapes and portraits
have, so to speak, their own personalities, and it is easy for the reproductive painter to mask his own lack of personality in the personality of things. But the cubist, stripping his object of all adventitious
aids to expressiveness, relying solely on the formal structure of his
straight lines and curves, surfaces and solid forms, is naked before the
world, revealed by the exact relationships he himself has determined.

TOUGH- AND TENDER-MINDED CUBISTS

    So clearly does the personality reveal itself in cubist painting,
that I think there is no difficulty in dividing the cubists themselves

[1] Cf. Rudolf Arnheim, 'Perceptual Abstraction and Art' *Psychological
Review*, vol. 54 (1947), p. 75: 'Form is sometimes considered a mere spice
added by the artist to the representation of objects in order to make it
pleasurable. Composition is often evaluated without any reference to the
subject expressed by it. In opposition to this view it must be asserted that,
in art as well as in general, form is an indispensable prerequisite for the
perceptual characterization of the content.'

into two schools, which we might, to adopt William James's terminology, call the tough-minded and the tender-minded. The tender-minded are those who, like Braque and Juan Gris, seem to carry their abstraction towards a decorative end. Their paintings are discreet in tone, carefully worked, plastically effective, related in their total effect to the still-life harmony of a painting by Chardin. They seem to carry with them some suggestion of the organic world, an undertone of vital processes. Far different are the tough-minded productions of a Léger, a Metzinger, a Duchamp or a Duchamp-Villon. All organic sensibility is suppressed. We are in a world of inorganic, of mechanic, sensibility. If there is an undertone, it is an undertone of the machine: the dynamo, the rock-drill, the hydraulic pump. This aspect of cubism is related to the movement known as constructivism.[1]

It is perhaps the most difficult aspect of cubism to accept. It is impossible that any person of real sensibility and unprejudiced mind could fail to be charmed in some way by a painting by Braque: it is a different matter with a painter like Léger. Here is no concession to sentiment, to charm, or to decorative function. Colour is often a discord, the form agitated and relentless. It is easy to dismiss such art as lacking in sensibility; and that, in effect, is what so good a friend to modern art as the late Roger Fry did in an article he once published.[2] He proceeded on the assumption that 'there is a real and profound antagonism between sensibility and mechanism'. But that is to limit unduly the meaning of the word sensibility. Roger Fry illustrated his meaning by reference to a drawing by Rembrandt of a sow. 'What happens to us when we are thrilled by the beauty of Rembrandt's drawing is that the peculiar rhythms of his lines transmit to us, not only the likeness of a sow, but also Rembrandt's imaginative excitement as he apprehended certain relations of form in what he contemplated, and that excitement and

[1] See below, p. 104n.
[2] 'Sensibility versus Mechanism', *The Listener*, vol. vii, No. 169, p. 497.

exaltation depended upon his peculiarly intense emotional reaction to life, an emotion expressed in his case through his specific sense of visible form.' But cannot I say something very similar about one of Léger's paintings? Cannot I say, to transpose Roger Fry's words: 'What happens to us when we are thrilled by the beauty of Léger's painting is that the peculiar rhythms of his lines and planes transmit to us, not so much the likeness of a town, but rather Léger's imaginative excitement as he apprehended certain relations of form in what he contemplated, and that excitement and exaltation depended upon his peculiarly intense emotional reaction to mechanism, an emotion expressed in his case through his specific sense of geometric form'? Is not that just as plausible as the description of Roger Fry's sensibility before Rembrandt's drawing? Must we not therefore conclude that we have, not a blank opposition between sensibility and mechanism, but rather an opposition between two kinds of sensibility? Cannot we have geometric as well as organic sensibility? The history of art proves that we can, abundantly. One may, of course, question the relative values of these two types of sensibility, but that they both have a natural existence is not to be denied.

MECHANIC SENSIBILITY

But we might ask why this mechanic or geometric sensibility should have a special appeal to-day, and I think the answer to that question will also give us a clue to the values underlying this form of sensibility. There are, I think, two answers to the question, one obvious enough, the other involving rather complicated questions of social psychology. The obvious ground for the appeal of mechanical forms is the presence in our daily life of so many machines: of so many objects, expressing in their lines and volumes a certain functional perfection to which we cannot deny the name of beauty. It is true, as Roger Fry points out, that all perfectly functioning machines are not beautiful: that the quality of beauty is perhaps confined to machines expressing some abstract notion like speed, power, or precision. But that does not alter the fact that we are surrounded by such examples of mechanical perfection, and that it would therefore seem legitimate to attempt to transfer to painting and sculpture the same qualities of perfection which we find expressed in machines.

But there is probably a profounder reason for the appearance of a mechanical or geometric sensibility in modern art, and that reason is the reason underlying all the recurrent phases of geometric art in history. There have been attempts to explain these phases on rationalistic grounds: various types of geometric ornaments are explained as developments of residuary technical elements. For example: the seams and stitches which were inevitable when man made vessels from sewn leather, were copied for decorative effect on similar vessels when made of clay. We have to imagine that man had become so used to these surface irregularities that he simply could not bear the sight of a smooth undecorated pot, and so he copied the accidental features of the earlier type on to the later type of vessel. There may, here and there in the history of art, be types which lend colour to such a theory, but it is inadequate to account for all types of geometrical art. It accounts for a few types of ornamental decoration, particularly in the Neolithic period: it does not account for the art of primitive man in general, for the geometric ornament of early Northern art, for the same element in Byzantine art, or many other types, including modern geometric art. We must look for some wider explanation in the spiritual life of the peoples concerned—for the science of art is finally the science of human psychology, and the mutations of the history of art are but part of the fundamental process governing all development in human history: 'the checkered, fateful adjustment of man to the outer world.'

This last phrase is quoted from Worringer's *Form in Gothic*, a work in which may be found a coherent psychological theory which includes in its scope the phenomenon of geometrical art. That principle, as it concerns us now, is first established in relation to the art of primitive man:

'For primitive man—still mentally undeveloped and therefore contemplating the chaos of the world surrounding him with timidity and doubt—artistic activity, as we have seen, had meant the impulse to establish another world of perceptual values, a world of absolute and permanent values placed above the shifting world of appearances and free from all the arbitrariness of life. He had therefore remodelled what was living and arbitrary in his ceaselessly fluctuating visual impressions into invariable symbols of an intuitive and abstract kind. His artistic will did not arise from the enjoyment of the direct, sensuous perception of the object; instead he created precisely in order to subdue the torment of perception, in order to obtain *fixed conceptual* images in the place of *casual perceptual* images. Consequently his art bore a positive, almost scientific character; it was the product of a direct impulse of self-preservation, not the unrestrained luxury product of a humanity delivered from all elemental world fears.'[1]

That is a succinct expression of what I believe to be the only theory that accounts at all adequately for the geometric, abstract nature of various types of art; and what I now want to suggest is, that there are conditions in modern life which give rise to a similar spiritual attitude in men, and to a similar expression of that attitude in art. We have, it is true, a mental equipment far different from that of primitive man; but is our outer world, in its state of political, economic and spiritual chaos, one which man can face with 'universal piety', sensuous satisfaction, spiritual aplomb? Is it not rather a world from which the sensitive soul, be he painter or poet, will flee to some spiritual reality, some sense of stability? And is he not likely, in that tendency, to desert the perceptual basis of the

[1] *Form in Gothic* (Eng. trans.), London, 1927, p. 29.

empirical art of the immediately preceding epoch, in favour of a fixed conceptual basis? There, at least, is a theory which would explain the origin, in our days, of a sensibility absolutely different in kind from the sensibility which Roger Fry gratuitously assumes to be the only kind of aesthetic sensibility. There is a spiritual satisfaction in such art which has nothing to do with the kind of emotional reaction to life which Rembrandt transmits; in Plato's words, it exists not relatively to anything else, but in its own proper nature, producing its own proper pleasures.

CONSTRUCTIVISM, PURE PLASTIC ART

The modern movement has evolved two or three types of geometric art, types that have a common origin but finally manifest distinct features. One such type arose in Russia in the years immediately preceding the First World War and was called *Suprematism*. In so far as it made use of industrial materials (steel, iron, glass, etc.) it was directly inspired by the functional ideals of a machine civilization (its chief theoretical exponent was Kasimir Malevich, 1878–1935). In so far as it aspired to independent aesthetic ideals Suprematism conformed in general to other types of abstract art, but two 'splinter groups' developed their own philosophical terminology. One of these was an offshoot of the Russian movement, led by the brothers Naum Gabo and Antoine Pevsner. Their work, mainly three-dimensional, is known as *Constructivism*. Another group arose independently in Holland as a development of the Jugendstil movement, and was known as *De Stijl*; from this group Piet Mondrian gradually detached himself and gave to his theory and practice the name *Neo-plasticism*. All these groups were related, either by a common philosophy of art or by the interchange of personalities, to contemporary developments in architecture and industrial design, of which the most significant was the Bauhaus which Walter Gropius directed at Weimar and Dessau from 1919–28.

The Bauhaus experiment was highly successful until disrupted by political catastrophe: it had a wide and decisive influence on the standards of design and construction both in Europe and America. The parallel movement in painting and sculpture provided an idealistic counterpart for the practical activities of the Bauhaus, but its philosophy (which in the case of Mondrian had mystical overtones derived from contemporary theosophy) was Platonic in the sense already indicated. The Constructivists used the word 'reality' to describe their ideals, but by this they wished to indicate that their aim was the creation of a *new* reality, the product of an activity using only the absolute elements of space and time—they even renounced colour as a pictorial means because of its 'accidental' nature. At the same time they maintained the humanistic significance of their activity: in the words of Gabo, the visual images created by the artist, though independent of science and technology, 'react on the common human psychology and transfer the artist's feelings to the feelings of men in general. Man's intuitive awareness of his own existence is 'the rock bottom of all human creations'.[1]

Mondrian was equally insistent on the social significance and 'realism' of his 'pure' plastic art. He announced that the culture of 'particular form' is approaching its end, and that the culture of 'determined relations' had begun. These determined relations are 'the great hidden laws of nature', hidden behind the superficial aspect of things. It is the function of abstract art to reveal such laws. Non-figurative art is seen as the final and supreme development of human culture—the realization of the one struggle of all art, which has always been to create universal beauty.[2]

---

[1] Cf. *Gabo: Constructions Sculpture Drawings.* London, 1957.
[2] Cf. *Plastic Art and Pure Plastic Art.* New York, 1945.

SOCIAL SIGNIFICANCE OF
GEOMETRIC ART

In accordance with this view of geometrical art in general, it is possible to regard the art I have described in this chapter as an art of despair—an art merely of escape from the complexity and confusion of modern life. There is, perhaps, this profound difference between the geometrical art of the past (such as Celtic art) and the geometrical art of to-day: that the one was done un-selfconsciously, in response to some spiritual impulse shared by the community, whilst to-day such art is conscious, prompted by the intellect, only appreciated by the intellect. That is not altogether true, for I hope I have shown that an emotional element is present in such art. But there is no doubt that the modern artist, feeling himself no longer in any *vital* contact with society, performing no *necessary* or *positive* function in the life of the community, retreats upon himself and gives expression to his own states of subjectivity, limiting himself to this expression, and not caring whether expression is also communication. In such a situation, once they realize it, many artists simply throw away their brushes and take to other work—to architecture, to journalism, even to commerce. Contemplating abstract paintings such as I illustrate, the plain man will probably conclude that they might have done worse. But let us be careful lest by encouraging this gesture of despair, this sabotage, we cut at the roots of the whole tradition of art. It may be true that the purpose of art cannot be achieved by artists individually. But if we examine the matter historically we shall be forced to admit that never since the Baroque period has art served a definitely collective purpose. All the art of the last 250 years is the production of individual artists. The work of art is a spot on the wall, a cabinet-picture for the delectation of the individual: the rest is reproduction and imitation. It is not for me to discuss the profound spiritual

[84]

causes underlying this historical change. They are causes which relate to the spiritual life itself—to the place of religion in the state and the practice of religion in the man: farther down than that, they relate to that delicate balance which man, if he is to remain vital, must always maintain between intellect and intuition, between knowledge and faith, between individuality and discipline. But I think it is false to take the long view *backwards*; nothing is so fatal to life as historical determinism, especially that grandiose and specious type associated with the name of Oswald Spengler. Art we should rather regard as an instrument in our hands, and our business, as artists and philosophers of art, is to keep that instrument sharp. Beyond that, we can only say that the artist is what we make him. But again I would insist that this does not mean that art in any fundamental sense is a mere reflex of social and economic conditions.[1] The *quality* of art is fairly constant, like the quality of all human products: that is why it is such a vulgar error to imagine that art in any essential sense is economically determined. But we must distinguish between the quality of art and the occasion of its exercise. Mozart was called upon to compose music for a mechanical toy, as well as for a religious mass. The quality of his genius was constant for both occasions; and that genius was not determined by the society in which Mozart lived. The modern painter is all the time composing for mechanical toys; but sometimes he does this so well, that we know he could if necessary build cathedrals.

[1] I have treated these difficult questions more adequately in *Art and Society* (3rd edn., Faber & Faber, 1956). See also p. 137–9 below.

Chapter V

SUPERREALISM (1)
ONEIRIC SYMBOLISM

THE THEORY OF AUTOMATISM

At the beginning of the last chapter I described the dilemma of the typical modern artist, the artist who has renounced the reproduction of the visible appearance of the object as an aim in art, and who then hesitates between abstraction and automatism. I went on to describe the theories underlying various modes of abstraction, and now, to complete the survey, I want to say something about two further, quite distinct, types of modern art that have a symbolic intention. One type makes use of dream imagery (oneiric symbolism), the other of informal imagery (calligraphic symbolism). Picasso may be taken as a point of departure for an exposition of the first type of symbolic art.

THE METHOD OF PICASSO

Picasso is an artist of many phases: he was one of the originators of the cubist school, and from time to time he makes excursions into the direct reproductive method of painting. But his most typical, and I think we can say his most consistent style is subjective. There are purer artists of this type, as I hope to show, but Picasso, by virtue of his energy, his experimental verve, his réclame, must be considered first. He himself has not been particularly

[86]

vocal, but a great deal has been written about him, and some of his *obiter dicta* have been reported.

To understand Picasso, and the whole of the school I am now going to deal with, one must admit as a simple preliminary a distinction between intuitive and rational modes of apprehension. I do not claim that the psychology of many of the apologists of Picasso and his school is particularly sound. It is rather vague. M. Zervos, for example, who has undertaken a comprehensive review of Picasso's work in several volumes, writes in this strain:

'Picasso has never set his will in opposition to his vision. . . . Vision is of quite a different order from will. The latter represents a continuous effort: intuition is a majestic leap into the unknown. One cannot attain the essence of things except by an extreme tension of the subjectivity.'[1]

Admittedly that sounds better in its original language, French; but terms like 'vision' and 'volonté' are dangerous terms to use without definition. Yet I think intuitive modes of apprehension are generally recognized in philosophy if not in psychology. It would be a poor philosophy that denied itself the evidence of the mystics; and even scientists like Poincaré and Einstein have admitted the intuitive nature of their thought processes. It is only by the acceptance of such an hypothesis that we can justify, or even explain, the art of a Picasso. Picasso himself relies on the distinction, and in a statement reported by M. Zervos, he makes this quite evident:

'I see', he confided to M. Zervos, 'for others; that is to say, so that I can put on canvas the sudden apparitions which force themselves on me. I don't know in advance what I am going to put on the canvas, any more than I decide in advance what colours to use. Whilst I work, I take no stock of what I am painting on the canvas. Every time I begin a picture, I feel as though I were throwing myself into the void. I never know if I shall fall on my feet again.

[1] *Cahiers d'Art*, Nos. 3–5, 1932.

It is only later that I begin to evaluate more exactly the result of my work.'

And M. Zervos, in continuation, explains the process in more detail:

'The moments of creation with Picasso are dominated by anguish. This anguish Picasso analysed for me recently. His only wish has been desperately to be himself; in fact, he acts according to suggestions which come to him from beyond his own limits. He sees descending upon him a superior order of exigencies, he has a very clear impression that something compels him imperiously to empty his spirit of all that he has only just discovered, even before he has been able to control it, so that he can admit other suggestions. Hence his torturing doubts. But this anguish is not a misfortune for Picasso. It is just this which enables him to break down all his barriers, leaving the field of the possible free to him, and opening up to him the perspectives of the unknown.'

I think that is as clear as we can expect a description of such subjective processes to be. We have to realize that we are now concerned, not with a logical development of the art of painting in Europe, not even with a development for which there is any historical parallel, but with an abrupt break with all tradition, with all preconceptions of what the art of painting should be. It would be much better if we could altogether abandon the word 'painting' for such an activity, but so long as it is an affair of canvas and paint, I am afraid that is too much to expect. Let us realize, however, that all links with the objective world are broken; that that love of the concrete which has characterized the art of Europe for centuries, and which has become inseparable from the very concept, is deliberately renounced. The painter instead turns all his perceptive faculties inwards, to the realm of his subjective fancies, his day dreams, his preconscious images. He replaces observation by intuition, analysis by synthesis, reality by superreality. If we can accept the hypothesis of the collective unconscious as formulated

PABLO PICASSO
Pêche de Nuit à Antibes

by Jung, it is even possible that an artist like Picasso is able to reveal those archetypal images which are its characteristic content.

PARALLELS IN MODERN MUSIC AND LITERATURE

Before trying to assess the consequences of this revolution, let us note that it is not confined to painting. We find experiments of precisely the same nature in both music and literature. The parallel in modern developments of music will be evident to those who are competent to deal with so complex a subject; it has been discussed with the greatest possible authority by Sir Donald Tovey.[1] The parallel in literature is even more exact, although, in my opinion, far less justified. The interior monologue, used as a method by James Joyce in *Ulysses*, is an attempt to transmit the flow of thought in all its subjective inconsequence direct to paper. We might say of such a method, and it is a distinction we may find useful in painting, that whilst the result, if honestly arrived at, will always have psychological value (as an individual case, at any rate), it will only have literary value in so far as it is justified by its literary technique, which always has an aesthetic motive (effective communication). In Joyce's case there is a positive lyrical value in the verbal texture of the monologue—if not always poetic, then at least witty. Such technical values distinguish this kind of literature from, shall we say, the case-histories in a psychological treatise; distinguish it, too, from those false imitations of Joyce which have neither his lyrical impulse nor his sense of wit. I speak here specifically of *Ulysses*. In the further experiments which Joyce has made (and again he has had many imitators) the dependence even on the inconsequent but still natural stream of consciousness is dispensed with, and a structure of words, entirely intuitive in their syntax and

[1] *Normality and Freedom in Music.* Romanes Lecture, 1936. (Oxford University Press.)

[89]

juxtaposition, is projected, very much in the same way that Picasso projects his plastic forms. Words become units almost as subjective in their effect as notes in music, and the result can only be received in its synthetic wholeness—it is in no sense logical.

Painting, which may be defined simply as the disposition of colours on a plane surface, can appeal to our senses directly, without the necessary intervention of visual images of the external world or of logical concepts, exactly in the same way that music does. There is therefore no *inherent* reason why painting should not be used to express the logically inexpressible. But what, in that case, is the nature of its appeal? Is it in any sense formal, even in the geometrical sense of form first advanced by Plato, and in our own time given literal expression by the Cubists?

THE CONCEPT OF FORM RE-EXAMINED

Before we can answer this question satisfactorily I think we must examine a little more closely the notion of *form*. We have already, in the previous chapters, employed the word in two senses. There is form in the *perceptual* sense, which, in Dr. Arnheim's words, is 'an indispensable prerequisite for the perceptual characterisation of the content.' There is, secondly, form in a *structural* sense: this is the classical conception of form: a certain harmonic or proportionate relation of parts to the whole and to each other which can be analysed and ultimately reduced to number. But there is still a third sense, which might be called Platonic, in which form is regarded as a representation of the idea. Form, in this sense, is *symbolic*, and may employ either naturalistic images, or alternatively, images of a non-naturalistic or non-figurative kind. The former type has often provided motives for artists in the past, either obviously, as when an Early Christian painter used the symbol of the Lamb, or more esoterically, as in a painting like Bellini's 'Christian Allegory' (see p. 93). We are now concerned with

[90]

symbolism of a much less conscious kind. Such symbolism is always a concretion of some kind: the discovery of an objective definite form to represent a vague, even a vast, field of subjectivity. But that definite form may in itself be very arbitrary, as in dream imagery, or very summary, as the Cross in Christianity, or the mandala in Oriental mysticism.

TWO TYPES OF SYMBOLISM

At this point it might assist the reader if I were to refer to an illustration of each type of symbolism. Plate 111, for example, is an abstraction by Picasso which has no parallel in visual experience. It would be difficult to argue that it had any harmonic or classical beauty. And yet, for some people, it has a strong appeal. It elicits some response in the unconscious; we like it as we might like a strange fungus, an orchid, a cloud-formation, a vein in marble. Plate 109 illustrates a painting by Dali which makes use of recognizable imagery, but it arranges it in an irrational manner for symbolic effect: what it symbolizes may not be evident: it may still be hidden in the unconscious. But there quite clearly we have two types of formal structure which do not correspond to perpetual experience, but depend for their appeal on unconscious factors.

It is true that in these illustrations the element of colour is eliminated: that merely simplifies the question for us. The element of colour may be a sensational quality in a form that is symbolic as form, and to that extent it complicates our analysis. But actually in this example the colour has no deliberate charm: it too is subordinate to the unconscious function of the projected image. The question that now arises is: is such symbolism in any sense aesthetic? There are people who intensely dislike any kind of association between symbolism and art. Roger Fry was one. In a paper on 'The Artist and Psycho-analysis'[1] he dealt with this very question.

[1] Hogarth Press, London, 1924, pp. 15–16.

[91]

He was speaking of symbolism of the kind that uses naturalistic imagery, and said, 'I come back to this, that nothing is more contrary to the essential aesthetic faculty than the dream. The poet Mallarmé foresaw this long before Freud had revealed the psychological value of dreams, for in his poem in memory of Théophile Gautier, he says, "the spirit of Gautier, the pure poet, now watches over the garden of poetry from which he banishes the Dream, the enemy of his charge." You notice that in this connection he calls him deliberately the pure poet, knowing that in proportion as poetry becomes impure it accepts the dream. . . . I have elsewhere expressed the belief that in a world of symbolists only two kinds of people are entirely opposed to symbolism, and they are the man of science and the artist, since they alone are seeking to make constructions which are completely self-consistent, self-supporting and self-contained—constructions which do not stand for something else, but appear to have ultimate value and in that sense to be real.

'It is, of course, perfectly natural that people should always be looking for symbolism in works of art. Since most people are unable to perceive the meaning of purely formal relations, are unable to derive from them the profound satisfaction that the creator and those that understand him feel, they always look for some meaning that can be attached to the values of actual life, they always hope to translate a work of art into terms of *ideas* with which they are familiar. None the less in proportion as an artist is pure, he is opposed to all symbolism.'

This, as I have already observed, is an attack on symbolism in a restricted sense, but even as such, I think it is a little too sweeping. Roger Fry himself went on to say that 'no-one who has a real understanding of the art of painting attaches any importance to what we call the subject of a picture—what is represented. To one who feels the language of pictorial form all depends on *how* it is presented, *nothing* on what'—a sentiment with which I entirely agree. But surely it rebounds against Roger Fry's own position, for a symbolic picture may still be a well-painted picture, expressing in every relation the artist's sense of *how*, as well as his care for the 'what'. I might give as an example Giovanni Bellini's 'Christian Allegory' from the Uffizi Gallery in Florence—a picture by an Italian master whom Roger Fry greatly admired. I am not sure, that in a picture like this, one so soon 'exhausts the feelings connected by associated ideas with the figures'—that 'what remains, what never grows less nor evaporates, are the feelings dependent on the purely formal relations'. Such was Roger Fry's objection to symbolist pictures in general, but surely there is bad symbolism and good symbolism, and though good symbolism will never justify a picture devoid of purely aesthetic values, yet granted these aesthethic values, good symbolism will prolong, deepen, and give significance to the pleasure we derive from a picture. Let us grant, however, that symbolism is an extremely dangerous language to use: that only the profoundest minds are capable of using it: that nothing is more desperately boring and distasteful than the misuse of it.

THE FUNCTION OF SYMBOLIC ART

Perhaps I might venture to indicate how symbolism in general produces a sense of pleasure, because I am quite willing to admit, that if we could separate the symbolic content of a picture like Bellini's from its formal content, then our reaction to the symbolism would not be strictly speaking *aesthetic*. 'Aesthetic' has acquired a special meaning, and is confined to modes of perception that affect our feelings of pain or pleasure. Art that is primarily symbolic can hardly be said to do this: it depends, not on an affective reaction at all, but on what I can only call recollection, a term I would like to introduce into the science of art. There is no doubt that an increasing number of people find in certain works of art, which in the

[93]

strict sense have no aesthetic appeal, a certain satisfaction which is neither intellectual nor sensational, but which must therefore be subconscious. The psycho-analytical theories of Freud and Jung give us plenty of justification for such a possibility: the artist, in short, becomes a man gifted with the capacity to project symbols from his unconscious, which symbols are of general validity—that is to say, they are symbols which other people might project if they had the capacity, and which, when projected for them, they can immediately accept. This act of acceptance replaces the feeling of pleasure which is the reaction in the case of a normal work of art. We might even go further and say that the values of such a type of art can be gauged by a new test of universality: universality on the plane of the unconscious.

From this point of view I am not sure that the formal values which Roger Fry expressly dissociates from symbolism are not in themselves symbolic. What is more, Roger Fry virtually admits it. At the conclusion of the paper from which I have already quoted he distinguishes the two types of form which I have called 'sensational' and 'intuitive'. He says:

'One thing I think we may clearly say, namely, that there is a pleasure in the recognition of order, of inevitability in relations, and that the more complex the relations of which we are able to recognize the inevitable interdependence and correspondence, the greater is the pleasure. . . . But in art there is, I think, an affective quality which lies outside that. It is not a mere recognition of order and inter-relation; every part, as well as the whole, becomes suffused with an emotional tone. Now, from our definition of this pure beauty, the emotional tone is not due to any recognizable reminiscence or suggestion of the emotional experiences of life; but I sometimes wonder if it nevertheless does not get its force from arousing some very deep, very vague, and immensely generalized reminiscences.—It looks as though art had got access to the substratum of all the emotional colours of life, to something which

[94]

underlies all the particular and specialized emotions of actual life. It seems to derive an emotional energy from the very conditions of our existence by its revelation of an emotional significance in time and space. Or it may be that art really calls up, as it were, the residual traces left on the spirit by the different emotions of life, without however recalling the actual experiences, so that we get an echo of the emotion without the limitation and particular direction which it had in experience.'

But this is just the perfect adumbration of the abstract kind of symbolism for which we are seeking! I am sorry to leave Roger Fry with little except symbolism, but that I think is what his essential in art amounts to. He has dismissed idea, he has dismissed symbolic imagery; he is left with the recognition of order (the classical concept of beauty) and with this other notion of form (which for clarity's sake we had better separate altogether from the concept of beauty) and this form is a concretion of some kind representing a vague, even a vast, field of subjectivity—which was precisely our definition of one kind of symbolism.[1]

SURRÉALISME

Picasso does not confine himself to the abstract type of unconscious symbolism, but the other type which makes use of recognizable imagery is more directly represented by a group of painters I have already referred to—the Surréalistes. The Surréalistes were preceded by a group known as the Dadaistes, but 'Dada' was anti-art; that is to say, it was the gesture of men too bored with the tragedy of life to be anything but irreverent. It was born at Zurich in 1916 and died at Paris in 1924. In 1924 'Surréalisme' rose from the ashes—and took definite shape in a manifesto issued by the poet André Breton. As a movement it is not confined to the plastic

[1] I have returned in much greater detail to the problem of symbolism in art in *The Forms of Things Unknown*. London and New York, 1960.

arts, but includes poetry, drama, and even psychology and philosophy; it has had somewhat unreciprocated affinities with communism in politics.

As the word implies, the main doctrine of the school is that there exists a world more real than the normal world, and this is the world of the unconscious mind. Though the Surréalistes acknowledge Lautréamont as their master (and his *Chants de Maldoror* is certainly a loaded mine of irrational fantasy), and even seek a metaphysical justification in the philosophy of Hegel, yet I doubt if 'Surréalisme' would ever have existed in its present form but for Sigmund Freud. He is the real founder of the school, for just as Freud finds a key to the perplexities of life in the material of dreams, so the 'Surréaliste' finds his best inspiration in the same region. It is not that he merely makes a pictorial representation of dream-images; his aim is rather to employ any means that will give him access to the repressed contents of the unconscious, and then to mingle these elements freely with the more conscious images and even the formal elements of the normal types of art. Surréalisme is not specifically an art of the unconscious—that would be too academic a conception of its aims. Surréalisme is an art without limits of any kind. Its underlying idea is the recovery, by means of what Breton calls 'a vertiginous descent into ourselves', of the whole force of the mental personality. It believes that there are hidden springs in the unconscious, and that these can be tapped if we give our imagination free rein—if we allow thought to be *automatic*.

As a movement, Surréalisme is totally distinct from all other contemporary schools, and indeed makes a complete break with all the accepted traditions of artistic expression. Inevitably, therefore, it arouses the bitterest opposition, not only in academic circles (generally content to dismiss it as an absurdity), but even from those painters and critics who are normally accepted as modernists. But such blind opposition has so often proved wrong in the past that we should at least make an attempt to understand the aim of

[96]

artists so sincere and determined as Max Ernst, Joan Miró and André Masson. All these artists show the same tendency towards what might be called a disintegration of the intellect or reason, which is one aspect of symbolism.

The artist, whether poet or mystic or painter, does not seek a symbol for what is clear to the understanding and capable of discursive exposition; he realizes that life, especially the mental life, exists on two planes, one definite and visible in outline and detail, the other—perhaps the greater part of life—submerged, vague, indeterminate. A human being drifts through time like an iceberg, only partly floating above the level of the consciousness. It is the aim of the Surréaliste, whether as painter or as poet, to try and realize some of the dimensions and characteristics of his submerged being, and to do this he resorts to the significant imagery of dreams and dream-like states of mind.

In an introduction to a book of Surréaliste engravings by Max Ernst (*La Femme 100 Têtes*), André Breton says that Max Ernst has the most magnificently haunted brain of to-day, and no one who knows that artist's work will be inclined to dispute the claim. But why be haunted? I think Mr Breton would reply that it is better than being bored. A statue, he says, which is quite devoid of interest in its proper place, becomes an object of wonder if put in a ditch. And so with existence in general: it is too dull in its proper place. It is the function of art to upset the apple-cart: to snatch things from the security of their normal existence, and put them where they have never been before, except in dreams.

Many critics, too occupied with the mysterious content of paintings such as Max Ernst's, do not stop to consider their aesthetic merits, and condemn them outright as being psychology or literature, anything but painting. Thereby such critics reveal their limitations, for, if for a moment they would forget the symbolism, they would discover (granted an unprejudiced sensibility) an endless charm in the colour and texture of the actual painting. For

Max Ernst is, perhaps in spite of himself, an artist in the accepted sense—a man who paints with taste and sensibility. He uses these gifts to convey his vision—his symbolic vision—just as Blake used his poetic sensibility to convey his symbolic vision. After a century or so we have arrived at the point of accepting the genius of Blake; in the same mood we shall one day accept the comparable genius of Max Ernst.

THE ART OF FREE FANCY: KLEE

The only other phases of modern art which we have not yet dealt with will now, I think, fit neatly into our categories. One such phase is again a symbolic art, but it is not symbolic in any of the senses we have already discussed. Nor is it in any way a reproduction of the direct experience of the eye (the phenomenal figure). It is an art of pure fantasy, and if it is objected that fantasy is a literary category, then it is literary art, but it is not ashamed of the fact. It is not devoid of formal values—no plastic art can be if it is to avoid disturbing effects on our sense of visual pleasure. But the formal element is quite subordinate to the content. The content is subordinate to nothing: it is free fancy. Paul Klee, the most representative artist of this type, has himself described his method of procedure by an allegory which shows the fanciful way in which his imagination works; we might call it 'Going for a walk with a line':[1]

'Let us, on the way constructing a topographical chart, make a short excursion into the land of better understanding. From a dead full-stop the first act of movement sets off. (Line.) After a short time a halt, to take breath (interrupted line, or line jointed by repeated halts). A look back, what a long way we have already gone (opposite movement). Then taking thought of the way hither and

---

[1] *Paul Klee*, by Leopold Zahn. Potsdam, 1920, pp. 19–20.

thither (bundles of lines). A river holds us up, we take a boat (wave movements). Further on a bridge appears (a series of arches).

'There we meet a like-minded person, who would also like to go and find greater knowledge. At first united by joy (convergence), but generally separated by differences (independent course of two lines). A certain excitement on both sides (expression, dynamism and psyche of the line).

'We cross a ploughed-up field (surface drawn through with lines), then a thick forest. The line loses its way, tries to find it and once even describes the classical movement of a running hound.

'I am no longer quite cool: in the vicinity of another river there is fog (spatial element). It will, however, soon become clear.

'Basket-makers are going home with their waggons (the wheel), with them a child with delightful curls (screw movements). Later it is sultry and dark (spatial element). Lightning on the horizon (zig-zag line), now stars above us (dots).

'Soon we reach our first lodging. Before going to sleep all kinds of recollections will emerge, because an excursion gives one so many impressions.

'All kinds of different lines, strokes, touches, smooth surfaces, speckled surfaces, hatched surfaces. Wavy motion. Restricted, jointed motion. Counter motion. Flecked, woven, walled, worn. Unanimity, community. The line petering out, getting strong again (dynamism).

'Happy symmetry of the first strokes, then restraints, nerves! Repressed trembling, flattery of hopeful little breezes. Brakes suddenly put on against the storm. Madness, murder.

'Good things as guide, the self in darkness and despair. The lightning is repeated in the fever-chart. A sick child. . . . All over.'

Klee's world is, in fact, a fairy world—an intellectual fairyland. It is, I think, a world quite different from any conceived by a Latin imagination: it is a world of spooks and goblins, of mathematical gnomes and musical imps, of elfish flowers and fabulous beasts: a

[99]

Gothic world. It reminds me strongly of certain kinds of mediaeval illumination, particularly the linear fantasies which decorate the Utrecht Gospels, but in general of the overflowing fun which we often find in mediaeval art. But the page of Klee's manuscript is, as it were, much larger: it is the open page of the imagination, the wider margin of what Freud calls the pre-conscious mind.

SYMBOLISM AND ABSTRACTION

Klee's art serves as a bridge between geometric abstraction and oneiric symbolism, between cubism and superrealism. His genius (like Picasso's) embraces the extremes of the modern movement, and at the same time transcends them. He has been claimed by the Surréalistes, but he never subscribed to their programme. He illustrates, better than any other artist of the period, the distinction I make between superrealism as a general phenomenon of our time, and the particular movement in art known as Surréalisme. As an ideology, Surréalisme has persistently but not successfully sought to place itself 'at the service of the Revolution'. In this respect it offers a contrast to the modern movement as a whole, and to superrealism as a wider phenomenon. Superrealism is essentially a poetic revolution, a continuation of the romantic tradition of subjectivism, but drawing new inspiration from the Freudian analysis of the unconscious. As such it might claim to have created a new mythology—it is a form of art which offers, that is to say, to provide for those needs which in less sophisticated ages found their expression in legend and folklore.

As for geometric art, which reached its logical extreme in the Neo-plasticism of Piet Mondrian, let it be admitted that although its pure values will always make a strong appeal to transcendental sensibilities—to those people who are willing to follow any of the arts in their approximations towards the aesthetic condition of music—yet on the other hand such art can never, in the present

[100]

condition of the world, be the only kind of plastic art. Indeed, though too strongly established to be in any danger of disappearance, geometric art will tend to separate off from the normal conception of painting and sculpture, both because there is no logical reason why it should be confined to the limited range of plastic materials implied by that conception, and perhaps because its energies will be absorbed by new developments in architecture and industrial design. Geometric art might well be called pure architectonics: it is the intuitive exploration and plastic statement of possible constructive values, and as such is far removed, not only from the humanistic elements which an artist like Picasso always retains, but also from the decorative values which even its critics are sometimes willing to concede to abstract art. To deny such an art a future is to deny something fundamental to all the arts.

Superrealism, in all but its party or political sense, includes such a wide diversity of styles—from the deliberately paranoiac fantasies of a Dali to the almost abstract harmonies of a Miró—that it would seem best to give the term the widest possible definition. By superrealism we could denote all forms of art which retain representational motives, but derive these, not exclusively from the level of the conscious ego, but *indifferently* from any level of the mental personality (assuming some such schematic division of the mind as that suggested by Freud[1]). The common notion of reality is based on the limited data of the conscious ego; superreality is a synthesis of experience which takes into account the evidence of every manifestation of mental life. How much the art of the past owes to the unacknowledged regions of the mind might easily be demonstrated. The fact that art now deliberately, or at least unashamedly, reckons with these sub- and super-conscious factors may so transform its force and function that art as we have known it may one day seem to have been but a prelude to art in its fullest sense.

[1] *New Introductory Lectures* (London, 1933), Lecture XXXI.

Chapter VI

SUPERREALISM (2)
NON-FIGURATIVE SYMBOLISM

FORMATIVE PROCESSES IN THE
UNCONSCIOUS

Superrealistic art of the type described in the last chapter presents an image which may be either oneiric (automatic or induced dream imagery) or formal (geometric or constructive). In both cases the intention is to present a symbol that is not only super-real, but also super-personal. The dream image of the Surréalistes attains its beatitude in the impersonal realm of the collective unconscious; the pure image of the neo-plasticist or the constructivist is, in Mondrian's words, 'unconditioned by subjective feeling and conception'.

After the Second World War there gradually emerged another type of superrealistic art that avoided both the figurative content of oneiric symbolism and the formal geometry of the constructive image. In theory if not in immediate inspiration this type of art returns to the abstract expressionism that Kandinsky had discovered in Munich in 1910. Such 'expression' proceeds from the personal unconscious and remains completely subjective in character. In order to understand the theoretical basis of this final phase of abstraction, it is desirable to take up the distinction we have already made between tough- and tender-minded cubists, which was based by William James on a much more fundamental distinction between two kinds of thinking—directed or logical thinking and fantasy thinking.

Directed or logical thinking, sometimes called reality-thinking, is *thinking in words*—it is, as Jung defines it, 'a thinking that is adapted to reality, by means of which we imitate the successiveness of objectively real things, so that the images inside our mind follow one another in the same strictly causal sequence as the events taking place outside it.' It has 'the peculiarity of causing fatigue, and is for that reason brought into play for short periods only.'[1]

'So long as we think directly, we think *for* others and speak *to* others.' But there is another kind of thinking which is non-directed, in which our thoughts seem to rise and sink according to their specific gravity. 'Much of our thinking,' says James, 'consists of trains of images suggested one by another, of a sort of spontaneous revery of which it seems likely enough that the higher brutes should be capable. This sort of thinking leads nevertheless to rational conclusions both practical and theoretical.'[2]

This type of thinking does not tire us. 'Image piles on image, feeling on feeling, and there is an ever-increasing tendency to shuffle things about and arrange them not as they are in reality, but as one would like them to be.'[3]

Dreaming, day-dreaming, the 'stream of consciousness' such as Joyce attempted to produce in *Ulysses*—these are types of non-directed thinking, and we know to what good use they have been put, creatively by poets and painters, analytically by psychiatrists.

Freud discovered that dreams had a tendency to *regress*—that is to say, to revert to the raw material of memory, mostly memory or early childhood. Jung believes that in our dreams and fantasy-thinking we regress even farther back, to the infancy of the race. Dream-thinking is the type of the primitive, pre-logical thinking of earlier stages of human culture. The myth is, as it were, 'a fragment

---

[1] *Symbols of Transformation* (London and New York, 1956), §11.
[2] *Principles of Psychology*, II, 325, quoted by Jung, *op. cit.*, 18.
[3] Jung, *op. cit.*, 19.

preserved from the infantile psychic life of the race, and dreams are the myth of the individual.'[1]

Psychoanalysts generally assume that not only ancient myths, but also all forms of art, ancient and modern, are a product not of calculation or of logical thinking but of non-directed thinking. What the psychoanalysts do not explain, or only explain very inadequately, is the formative process clearly discernible in all true works of art. A dream may be incoherent and its incoherence can be explained only by exposing some hidden cause—some suppressed experience or wish. But works of art are usually coherent: they are 'composed', and the question we must ask is how do such works of art become composed without involving faculties that are rational and logical—faculties inconsistent with the non-directed process of fantasy-thinking. Is it possible that fantasy itself, as a symbolic discourse, a language of icons or images, can also be 'directed'?

This is the difficult point. If we think of such 'direction' as an act of will, as conscious, then we are lost. We have to adopt, rather, the technique familiar to the ancient Chinese philosopher, and to a certain extent to Western mystics like Master Eckhart, the art of letting things happen, of action in non-action. Of this Jung says: 'The key is this: we must be able to let things happen in the psyche. For us, this becomes a real art of which few people know anything. Consciousness is forever interfering, helping, correcting, and negating, and never leaving the single growth of the psychic processes in peace. It would be a simple enough thing to do, if only simplicity were not the most difficult of all things. It consists solely in watching objectively the development of any fragment of fantasy.'[2]

That is the process adopted by the painters we are now going to discuss—they watch *objectively* the development of a fragment of

[1] Abraham, *Dreams and Myths*: quoted Jung, *op. cit.*, 29.
[2] *Secret of the Golden Flower* (London, 1938), p. 90.

fantasy, and once they have recorded this development, then criticism may afterwards develop and the fantasy may be interpreted or, as Jung suggests, 'aesthetized'. But the essential form has been developed in the unconscious—the conscious aestheticization of this form is the conscious control of the *means* of expression—the line and colour, the *facture* of the painting.

As Jung and other modern psychologists are willing to confess, there is much that goes on in the depths of the unconscious of which we still have no adequate knowledge. I am convinced that in the deeper layers of the unconscious there is a formative principle at work, moulding some primordial material of the psyche into icons. I prefer to call them icons rather than symbols, because the word symbol is ambiguous. An icon is an image wrought out of the *materia primordialis* of the unconscious and its purpose is to provide an objective correlative—an object with apprehensible form and colour—that answers to an internal necessity. We may never be able to define this necessity—to define it would be to indulge in directed thinking, in words, whereas this process is confined to shapes or forms. It is not, however, a merely automatic process, like dreaming or myth-making. The artist begins with a background that is mysterious, unformed, and this he may actually prepare automatically by scribbling or doodling with his paintbrush. But then he begins to elaborate, to delineate, never resorting to logical or verbal processes, but nevertheless proceeding by purposive steps—one stroke or spot determining the shape and place of the next stroke or spot; until finally he is left with an image whose origins or significance he cannot explain (and does not desire to explain) and yet which constitutes for him something valid, something *true*, something deeply necessary, a vital 'presence'. We cannot give it a meaning in the sense we give a meaning to a word or to a sign. Indeed, for all we know it may signify many things, and be a different thing to different people. We know that certain images have passed from religion to religion, and have been given different signification in each—the cross is an example. But the image in question may possess all these possibilities of interpretation all the time, and be most potent when we do not attempt to reduce it to any one of them.[1]

The new developments in painting now in question are all forms of art determined by internal necessity—by the need to project, as fantasy-thinking or symbolic discourse, a psychic activity that is distinct from logical thinking. I believe that this type of art is quite different from the super-real types of art already discussed. Michel Tapié has rightly called this new art 'un art autre', a new kind of art.

AN ART OF INTERNAL NECESSITY

The Surréalistes, as we have seen, practised automatism in art, but they were mainly interested in the automatic projection, or the uncontrolled recording, or dreams and unconscious fantasies. As the name indicates, such an art is an inverse realism. It takes a given material—in this case, the symbolic images that constitute our dream-world—and attempts to record this material by methods that are identical with those of realist art. That is to say, it attempts to present dream images clearly, to establish their precise limits. Surrealist painters like Dali and Tanguy, Magritte and Delvaux, were not merely painters in the realist tradition—they even adopted the most academic technical standards of that tradition. They often did this in a perverse, mocking spirit, but their serious concern was to delineate symbols accurately, and they were prepared to use any illustrative technique—they would have used photography if that

---

[1] Cf. Mircea Eliade, *Images et Symboles*, (Paris, 1952), pp. 13–14: La pensée symbolique n'est pas le domaine exclusif de l'enfant, du poète ou du déséquilibré: elle est consubstantielle à l'être humain: elle précède le langage et la raison discursive. Le symbole révèle certains aspects de la réalité—les plus profonds—qui défient tout autre moyen de connaissance. Les images, les symboles, les mythes, ne sont pas des créations irresponsables de la psyché; ils répondent à une nécessité et remplissent une fonction: mettre à nu les plus secrètes modalités de l'être.

had been scientifically possible, but we have not yet invented an X-ray apparatus to photograph our dreams.

One of the side-shows of Surréalisme was the *objet trouvé*. The 'object' might be an oddly marked or oddly shaped stone; a piece of sea-worn timber or a gnarled root; a piece of scrap-iron or a clinker—it was picked up and carefully mounted and piously exhibited. Like the blotches on a wall that Leonardo recommended the artist to study for indication of subject and composition; or like the blots used in the Rorschach Test, such objects had a power of suggestion, even a magical or sinister quality. This attraction could not be explained—in fact, to interpret such an object was to destroy its fascination. Much better to regard it as a fetish, an object to be feared or respected.

This experience with natural objects led to the deliberate creation of objects with a similar potency. I say 'deliberate', but it was recognized that chance was of the essence of such objects, and that no human effort could guarantee their 'magic'. The art of painting —or of mixing concrete or casting metal, for all creative methods are permissible as long as they result in a strange shape—must be spontaneous or naïve. It must be the unimpeded expression of the artist's temperament—like the scribbling of an infant, like a child's finger-painting.

Kandinsky's first abstract paintings had been preceded in his development by paintings of the 'Fauve' type—that is to say, expressionistic studies of landscapes and street scenes, vigorous in treatment and violent in colour. There were earlier phases of a realist and an impressionist character, but these do not concern us except that they show the naturalistic origins of Kandinsky's style. The *fauve* paintings of 1908–9 are gradually simplified: details are suppressed and in the end, that is to say, by about 1912, we can only vaguely distinguish a tree or a rock or a building in a composition which is not cubist, in the manner of the contemporary paintings of Picasso and Braque, but still distinctly organic and vitalistic.

AN ART OF INTERNAL NECESSITY

In an article in the *Burlington Magazine* (June, 1957)[1] Lorenz
Eitner has shown that Kandinsky's break-through to non-objective
painting occurred fairly suddenly: 'The increasing abstraction in
Kandinsky's landscapes and figure compositions does not lead to
it directly, nor is it the gradual emancipation of colour from descriptive meaning that brings it about. Totally non-objective
shapes are found first in studies of primarily graphic character,
rather than in colour compositions. The Münter Collection includes several such drawings in pen and ink or in pencil. Their
criss-crossing lines, some spidery and sharp, some softly blurred,
shoot across the paper singly or in tangles, like the traces of sudden
energy discharges, suggestive only of motion or tension, not of
body'. The inspiration for these exercises, Eitner suggests, may
well have come from *art nouveau* ornament—as indeed did the inspiration for Mondrian's non-objective art. Eitner further remarks
that Kandinsky's interest in 'primitive' art and in the spontaneous
drawings of children may also have played a part. 'Several of these
purely non-objective designs are washed with diluted ink or water-
colours. This strikingly alters their effect. The lines become con-
tours, the spaces between them take on substance, the compositions
turn into arrangements of fragmented but tangible matter'.

Kandinsky does not seem to have carried non-objective design
into oil-painting until about 1913, though he seems to have been
aware of the possibility in 1910, when he wrote his treatise *Con-
cerning the Spiritual in Art* (it was not published until 1912). There
he clearly distinguishes the evolutionary stages that had led him to
non-objectivity. I quote from the conclusion of his book; he says:

'I have added reproductions of four of my own pictures. They
represent three different sources of inspiration:

[1] His article is based on the Münter Collection now in the Städtische
Galerie of Munich—a collection which consists of a large quantity of
material left in his studio by Kandinsky in 1914 and preserved intact by
his friend Gabriele Münter.

(1) A direct impression of nature, expressed in purely pictorial form. This I call an "Impression".

(2) A largely unconscious, spontaneous expression of inner character, non-material nature. This I call an "Improvisation".

(3) An expression of a slowly formed inner feeling, tested and worked over repeatedly and almost pedantically. This I call a "Composition". In this, reason, consciousness, purpose, play an overwhelming part. But of calculation nothing remains: only feeling.'

These words of 1910 were prophetic, for they are an anticipatory description of all the main varieties of modern art. Even those post-Second World War tendencies which are our present concern can be grouped under the heading of 'improvisation'.

In the more theoretical part of his treatise of 1910, Kandinsky warned us of two dangers to which many painters subsequently succumbed, and also defined more precisely what he meant by 'improvisation'. The first danger, Kandinsky suggested, was 'the completely abstract use of colour in geometrical form (danger of developing into purely external ornamentation) pure patterning'. I will not stop to discuss this prophecy, which was to be amply fulfilled in the development of an academic non-figurative art. I would merely remark, in passing, that one of the most difficult tasks of contemporary art criticism is to distinguish between a constructive and an ornamental use of abstraction. The second danger mentioned by Kandinsky has also been incurred—'a more naturalistic use of colour with concrete form (danger of shallow fantasy)'. I am not sure what Kandinsky meant here: in a footnote he says that 'the new naturalism will not only be equivalent to but identical with abstraction'. But from what he wrote elsewhere I think he meant to warn us against the return to a symbolic use of colour such as had prevailed in the Middle Ages, and of which Gauguin was the contemporary example.

Having uttered these warnings, Kandinsky goes on to make a

statement which not only explains the kind of painting he himself was attempting at the time, but foreshadows the more recent developments of painting that are my immediate concern. He suggests that we are experiencing one of the great germinative periods in the history of art, and that artists are moved by a great compulsive force, an 'internal necessity'. The natural forms which had been the concern of conventional art represent impediments to the free expression of this internal necessity and they must be set aside. New constructions corresponding to the artist's inner compulsion must be developed—what we now call, after Mr. Eliot, 'objective correlatives.' Cubism, which was the experiment in this direction being carried out at the time Kandinsky was writing, was a transitional phase in which natural forms were forcibly subjected to a geometrical construction; this, said Kandinsky, was a process which tends to hamper the abstract by the concrete and spoil the concrete by the abstract—in other words, cubism was a compromise.

What is necessary, Kandinsky went on to say, is a form of art appealing less to the eye and more to the soul; not obvious geometrical constructions, but forms (configurations) emerging unnoticed from the canvas. Such 'concealed constructions' may be composed of 'seemingly fortuitous shapes, without apparent connection. But the outer absence of such a connection is proof of its inner presence'. What externally seems to be a lack of cohesion may represent an internal harmony. Those 'somehow' related forms are actually very precisely bound together. In this direction, concluded Kandinsky, lies the future structure of painting.

He warned his readers, however, that the achievement of an objective correlative in painting was no easy task. It would need the co-operation of 'rational factors', by which Kandinsky meant an objective knowledge of the craft. It is perhaps not necessary to remind the reader that Kandinsky himself was a master of all the scientific aspects of picture making.

Kandinsky's own future development was to be dominated by 'reason, consciousness, purpose'. He gradually discarded the 'largely unconscious, spontaneous expression of inner character, non-material nature', but calculation remained. In the article I have already quoted, Mr. Eitner points out that one of the important lessons which the Münter material yields is 'the realization that Kandinsky planned his own compositions with extraordinary care. It is clear that, before touching brush to canvas, he was able to visualize these involved configurations with the utmost precision. Every detail and the disposition of the whole were minutely predetermined. We learn to our surprise that apparently 'accidental' shapes, the merest blobs and scrawls, actually developed from careful studies; the Münter material includes drawings in which seemingly trivial details are rehearsed over and over again. Nothing could be less true than the view which sees in these compositions an orgy of emotional expressionism. They have little or nothing in common with Dada automatism or so-called action painting. Kandinsky composed as methodically as Ingres. His non-objective paintings are admirable feats of intellectual concentration; they were made possible by an unusually precise visual imagination and a phenomenal visual memory'.

This comment perhaps fails to distinguish between fantasy-thinking and logical thinking. Though Kandinsky's method was deliberate, it was not verbalized. A precise visual imagination can be animated by processes of formation in the unconscious—indeed, such a precise imagination is necessary to realize the shapes suggested by fantasy.

ABSTRACT EXPRESSIONISM

At the time Kandinsky was writing his *Spiritual Harmony*—1910 —Freud's theory of the unconscious was already formulated, but its general application to cultural problems was not known. *The*

Interpretation of Dreams was first published in Vienna in 1900, but was scarcely noticed. *Totem and Taboo*, which initiates Freud's more general applications of his theory, was not published until 1912, the same year as Kandinsky's book. I mention these facts to show that there was no particular reason why Kandinsky should make use of the terminology we now find so apt: in particular, the concept of the unconscious. When Kandinsky speaks of 'the largely unconscious, spontaneous expression of *inner character, non-material nature*', he is indeed referring to what we would now call the unconscious. But there is some ambiguity at this point: do we mean that the process of expression itself is unconscious—that is to say, non-directed; or do we mean that what is expressed—the inner character or non-material nature of what is expressed—is pre-formed unconsciously? We should draw a distinction nowadays between spontaneity or automatism, an act of *projection*, and what is prior to projection, an act of *formation* or *creation* that takes place below the level of consciousness.

But how does such unconsciously formed material become expressed? The most normal method is, of course, by dreaming. We also express our unconscious in habits, in gestures, in tics, in habitual phrases, in word-associations—in the many little ways which only the trained psychiatrist can detect. But all these are non-directed modes of expression, and what we are trying to discover is whether there is any method by means of which we can become more conscious of the forms that lie below the level of consciousness. But what is below the level of consciousness is no simple dream-world of measurable boundaries: it is rather a seething cauldron, as Freud calls it; and what may float to the top of this cauldron is not necessarily of the same nature as what sinks to the bottom. It is like Dante's Inferno, with spirals descending into the depths, until they are lost in total obscurity.

What emerges from this Inferno may be good or may be bad—there is no moral criterion for the unconscious; it may be beautiful

BEN NICHOLSON
Still Life, Zennor Head

or ugly—there is no aesthetic criterion for the unconscious; it may be personal or impersonal—there is no individuality in the unconscious: we do not dream—we are dreamed. But what is important from our point of view is the fact that there is no natural or rational order in the unconscious—there is a network of complexes, without form or affective organization. It is only as the unconscious emerges to the level of consciousness—and the remembering of a dream is already an effort of consciousness—it is only then that the contents of the unconscious take on significant form, and may as a consequence set up emotional reactions when we contemplate them.

The unconscious, though it controls our conscious lives to an extent we never fully realize, is accommodated—that is to say, made acceptable to our consciousness—by a process which Freud called the reality-principle. Freud was thinking mainly of the accommodation of sexual instincts to social conventions, to morality. I am not going to dispute the pan-sexuality of Freud's theory: it does not matter from our present point of view whether or not the forms that emerge from the unconscious are sexual: we are concerned only with their configuration (*Gestalt*). The fact we begin from, as artists, is the existence of an 'internal necessity', an 'inner need', a compulsive will to seek the expression of we know not what; and as artists what we seek is a concrete form—a configuration in colour or sound or even words—that will correspond to this need, and by objectifying it, defining it, clarifying it, leave us in a condition of inner calm, of psychic equilibrium.

We are born with this need for expression—the infant cries as soon as it is born, and begins to express its inner needs in a hundred ways. Admittedly these needs are mainly somatic, visceral, excretive; but they are also emotional—the need for love, for example; and we now realize that the youngest infant is creative within its own means of expression. By this I mean that there exists, from the beginning, a need to find an objective correlative—an external 'thing' which we create, own, take pride in, and correlate with our obscure states of feeling. The Freudians point out that the child's faeces are the first expression of this kind—objects, as Freud says, which 'produce no disgust in [the infant]; he values them as part of his own body and is unwilling to part with them, he uses them as the first "present" by which he can mark out those people whom he values especially.'[1] That kind of expressive activity is soon repressed, and there appear various substitute activities, mostly in the form of play.[2]

Scribbling is a natural activity in children, and recently an American teacher, Mrs. Rhoda Kellogg, has made a study of more than 100,000 drawings and paintings made by children of two, three and four years of age. She found that there is a definite sequence of development from scribbling to drawing, and that scribbling is not the aimless activity we had supposed. She was able to distinguish 20 basic scribbles, several of which may be found mixed in any one example of a child's early scribbling activities; and out of these scribble-mixtures there emerge six basic diagrams (Greek cross, square, circle, triangle, the odd shaped area and the diagonal cross). These basic diagrams are at first difficult to distinguish in a confused area of scribbling, but they begin to emerge more and more definitely, and are then combined—a Greek cross is combined with a diagonal cross, or with a square; circles are aggregated and combined with squares and crosses; and what finally emerges is that archetypal form, the mandala, represented schematically as a cross within a circle. From this simple abstract form, by gradual variations, a diversity of pictorial symbols is evolved.

---

[1] *Introductory Lectures*, 1922, p. 265.
[2] The fact that such modes of expression are substitutes for the faeces does not mean that they are developments from the faeces. The faeces are used because the faeces are there, and because the child had not yet developed the muscular co-ordination for other means of expression. But when, between the age of two and three, the child can hold a crayon and by tracing his gestures, objectify his inner needs in visible and viable marks, then he acquires a completely new means of expression.

I do not mention these facts for their educational interest, important as that is; but rather to show that the path of development followed by the artists we are now considering is virtually the same. They begin with basic scribbles, and by elaborating them, concentrating them, extract from the primordial confusion an archetypal form. It is possible to find among the scribble diagrams produced spontaneously by children, prototypes of most of the types of contemporary painting that are our immediate concern. Though some of these paintings are by intention calligraphic (Hartung, Mathieu, Soulages, Kline), it does not follow that we can dismiss them as infantile. Not only is there a difference of scale and manipulative skill, but also there does intervene, as I intend to show, an element of direction, of control, of personal involvement.

ACTION PAINTING

There are degrees, and even differences in kind, of automatism. The dream activity, as has often been pointed out, cannot properly be described as automatic: it is determined either by pre-existing complexes, or by somatic stresses. The projection of a dream may possibly be 'automatic', in the sense that there is no intervention of the conscious will—that was the ideal of the Surréalistes. The scribbling of children is automatic in another sense—an uncontrolled motor activity which may nevertheless develop symbolic significance. Certain Surréalistes interpreted automatism in this way—notably André Masson and Joan Miró—and it was this subspecies of Surréalisme that was to lead to a new movement in the United States to which the name of action-painting has been given.

This type of automatism might be compared to a highly sophisticated form of scribbling—for example, to Oriental calligraphy, and actually Oriental calligraphy, in the case of artists like Henri Michaux and Mark Tobey, has been a direct influence. But calligraphy, even in the cruder form of our alphabetic handwriting, represents a developed skill: it is only automatic in the sense that we have forgotten the learning process. If the signature of an adult is automatic, then the scribble of a child should perhaps be called instinctive.

The linear ecstasies practised by Masson around 1941, in which year he became a refugee in the United States, are sophisticated or stylized calligraphy, evidence of long training in brush-work; so were the early improvisations of Kandinsky. When Jackson Pollock began to paint in the style of Masson and Miró, he was adopting the stylized calligraphy of these forerunners, and there was nothing naïve or childlike about his activity. His originality, as Harold Rosenberg has pointed out,[1] consists in the fact that he so increased the scale and continuity of his calligraphic gestures that the canvas became 'an arena in which to act—rather than a space in which to reproduce, re-design or "express" an object, actual or imagined. What was to go on the canvas was not a picture but an event'. The aim was no longer 'self-expression', or even the automatic projection of formal elements of unconscious origin: 'the new painting is of the same metaphysical substance as the artist's existence'. In this manner the reproach of Hannah Arendt (see page 68 above) is avoided: 'Action Painting has to do with self-creation or self-definition or self-transcendence; but this dissociates it from self-expression, which assumes the acceptance of the ego as it is, with its wound and its magic'.

The necessity is no longer 'internal', no longer 'spiritual' in Kandinsky's sense of the word. Harold Rosenberg would argue that the resulting gesture is no longer aesthetic—'Form colour, composition, drawing, are auxiliaries, any one of which . . . can be dispensed with.' This generalization would not be accepted by all those who have been labelled action painters; their work in effect is as various as their personalities, and the detached observer would

---

[1] *The Tradition of the New*. New York, 1959.

rather conclude with Alfred Barr that 'in spite of their intransigence, their following increases, largely because the paintings have a sensuous, emotional, aesthetic and at times mystical power which works and is overwhelming'.[1]

THE CLOUD OF UNKNOWING

Freud, as I have said, described the unconscious as a seething cauldron. Visually such a cauldron would present an agitated heaving surface from which, from time to time, objects of a definite shape would appear to float for a moment and then sink. Some of the painters I have referred to would seem to be trying to represent such a bubbling surface. Generally speaking the European 'tachiste', in so far as he is distinct from the American 'action painter', is searching for a simulacrum rather than making a gesture of self-definition: he believes that he is depicting an objective reality, of which he is the channel but not the source. He manipulates his 'blot', his tache, until it begins to correspond with his intuition of this objective reality. But the reality is never static.

The title of the fourteenth century mystical treatise, the *Cloud of Unknowing*, would fit some of the paintings of Sam Francis or Mark Tobey. But the clouds are moving, swirling, and among them are certain more definite forms, the 'shapes that haunt thought's wildernesses.' The poet, says Shelley, draws his inspiration from a shifting cosmic panorama, from a 'boundless element' through which forms voyage 'cloudlike and unpent'. Kandinsky used similar expressions—he spoke of 'the symphony of forms that arises from the chaotic hubbub of cosmic elements which we call the music of the spheres'. The latest picture of the universe offered to us by the astronomists is of an infinite explosion of matter, a state

[1] Introduction to *The New American Painting*, catalogue of an exhibition by the International Program of the Museum of Modern Art, New York, 1959.

of continuous creation and destruction, within which, however, we discover nuclei of form and structure, constellations and finite worlds, and within these, the infinite recession of perfect forms.

The type of artist we are considering is searching for similar forms behind the veil of consciousness, for forms irrespective of any representational significance, that can be teased out of the seething cauldron of psychic particles. Such forms need not be figurative: they are more likely to be amorphous, 'gestaltlos'. The deeper we penetrate the cloud of unknowing, by contemplation and intuition, the less likely are we to find the shapes and images of our waking world. We enter a 'Gestalt-free matrix of forms', as Anton Ehrenzweig has called it, a matrix within which the shapes are as yet unformed, and only acquire form and significance as the inchoate primary substance coagulates, so to say, on the painter's canvas in the act of painting. He searches the tenuous limits of his awareness with brush in hand: he manipulates the paint until a significant form begins to emerge. It may emerge almost instantly, or it may have to be slowly teased out of the cloud of unknowing, out of thought's wildernesses. How does a painter recognize a significant form? Why does he stop at one particular moment and cry: I have found it! Why is one particular form more significant than another? To these questions I think that at present we can only answer: because such forms, when found, are potent—they exercise a power, first of all on the painter, and then, when exhibited, on the spectator.

To explain this power the word 'magic' has again been evoked. It is not a word to be used if it implies some notion of occult forces, or spiritual agencies, which are certainly not present in the work of the painters we are discussing. But I think it is legitimate to use the notion of an archetypal form, that is to say, of a process of crystallization that takes place without the intervention of the conscious will, and leaves us with a shape, more or less complex, that appeals to us for reasons more or less unknown. I say 'more or less unknown' because although it is sometimes possible to read sexual symbolism into such shapes, in most cases the symbolic function of the forms remains indeterminate.

I would like to suggest that it is not necessary to search irritably for an interpretation of such forms. We can admire Mexican or Peruvian works of art without possessing any knowledge of the symbolic function of these works in the lost religions of those civilizations. We can admire prehistoric and oriental works of art whose meaning and purpose are equally unknown to us. Among such works are also archetypal forms, appealing to us not only by virtue of their proportion and harmonies, but also because the forms themselves have a mysterious potency that is super-real and non-aesthetic. It may be that the impression they create is in some sense vitalistic; but anthropology has also given us the word 'animistic', which I prefer to 'magical' because it does not necessarily imply an occult power operating on us, but merely the presence, in the object, of a vital principle, a living 'soul.' Again, I do not suggest the application of an anthropological term to the creations of the modern artist: the vital principle which they embody is the artist's own—a vitality inspired by his own breath, the progeny of his own spiritual being. Among the several words that have been suggested (mainly by French critics) as descriptive of these 'animistic' forms I myself prefer 'presence'—it indicates a configuration (*Gestalt*) with a distinctive individuality. A painting by Fautrier, Wols, or Sam Francis may be indeterminate, almost indefinable: a coagulation of irregular blotches with scarcely an outline to delimit it, except the edge of the canvas. And yet, out of the volcanic surface, emerges a presence. There is a man in the moon!

CONCLUSION

It is necessary to end this chapter (and this book) on a note of warning. I have spoken of automatism and I have perhaps given the impression that in order to produce paintings of the kind I have described it is only necessary to hold a paint-brush in one's hand and trust to luck. This is far from being the case. Painting remains a craft, a technique to be mastered, the product of discipline. I have mentioned the fact that Kandinsky, who might be called the first master in this new school of painting, was a highly conscious craftsman: his paintings exhibit great skill, great science. The same can be said of Klee and Picasso. There is no escape in art (and why should there be?) from the few but exacting conditions that determine the effectiveness of the means employed. The end may determine means which another age would reject: we no longer appreciate enamel-like surfaces and sweet harmonies of tone. Dissonance and conflict have become essential elements in our aesthetic experience. But always the artist must proceed with the fullest possible equipment; and it is particularly essential that a mode of procedure that involves observing and recording the subtlest intuitions of the sensibility should not be hampered by clumsiness and inefficiency. 'Internal necessity' is perhaps the key phrase in the art of our time; but to this internal necessity corresponds an external necessity, which is simply the necessity to communicate with other people with the maximum intensity; and art is the reconciliation of these two necessities.

INDEX

(a) *General*

A.B.C. de la Peinture (Sérusier),
  49 n
Abraham, 104
Abstract art: Mondrian on function
  of, 83
Abstract expressionism, 102–3,
  111–15
'Abstract idea' made out by artist,
  of forms more perfect than nature
  (18th-century classicism), 24
Abstract impressionism, *see* Kandinsky
Abstraction, theory of, 69–85; Kandinsky's discovering of, 67;
  Cézanne's approach to, 74–5;
  Plato's anticipation of, 72–4;
  and Symbolism, 100–1
Academic tradition, break-up of,
  43 seqq.; as 'what the eye sees',
  45–7; 'academic' standards of
  surréalistes, 106
'Action in non-action', 104
Action painting, 115–17
Aesthetics: based on empirical
  study of works of art, 30 seqq.;
  aesthetic experience before work
  of art, three stages of, 36–7;
  aesthetic phase in human development, notions of essential
  nature of, 22, 28, 29; aesthetic
  sensibility, development of basic
  to development of reason and
  morality, 22 seqq.; aesthetic values, intellection and judgment no
  part of, 38; Baumgarten's claim
  for, and definition of, 26; sympathy as basis of aesthetic enjoyment, 36
Alberti, 24
Allen, Grant, 30
Anfänge der Kunst (Grosse), 32
Apollo of the Belvedere, 29

A priori principles, 71, 74, Ch. 1
  passim
Aquinas, Thomas, 73, 75
Archetypal forms, 115, 118, 119
Architectonic unit (Classical Renaissance, Cézanne), 57
Arendt, Hannah, 68, 116
Aristotle—Scholastic philosophy—
  Vico link, in genetic concept, 24–
  26
Aristotle, 24, 25, 45, 73, 74
Arnheim, Rudolf, 77 n
Art: as basis of education, 27;
  changes in philosophy of: *a
  priori* method yields to new
  science of art, 21; new fields
  supplying evidence for this
  science, 21; 18th-century
  'science of art', 21; theory of
  abstraction and automatism, 72
  seqq.; biological and sociological
  function of, 39; Celtic, 84; of
  children, *see* Children; contemporary chaos of, 43; creative
  process (visual), 5 stages of, 37;
  as evolution of analysis of vision,
  56; creative aspect of, 37–8; as
  'will creative in terms of a
  material' (Riegl, Fiedler), 31; of
  free fancy, 98–100; and function,
  35; genetic concept of (Vico),
  24–6; geometric types of, 75–6,
  79–85, 100, 101; Hegel's principles basically hostile to, 29; as
  stage in ideal history of mankind,
  26; as interpretation of reality,
  41; of internal necessity, 105,
  106–11; 'literary', 59 seqq.;
  modern dilemma in, 71, 86;
  non-figurative, Mondrian sees as
  supreme development of human
  culture, 83; point of departure,

[121]

(b) *Plates*

1. CÉZANNE (1839–1906)
Mont Ste. Victoire, 1904–06
Photo: Alex. Reid & Lefèvre, Ltd.

2. CÉZANNE
Boy wearing a straw hat. 1896
Photo: Wildenstein

3. HENRI MATISSE (1869-1954)
Portrait of a girl in a yellow dress. 1929-31
Etta Cone Collection, Museum of Art, Baltimore, U.S.A.

4. HENRI MATISSE
Odalisque with chair. 1928
Photo: Bernheim jeune

5. OSKAR KOKOSCHKA (b. 1886)
The Wind's Bride (Tempest) 1914
Kunstmuseum, Basle

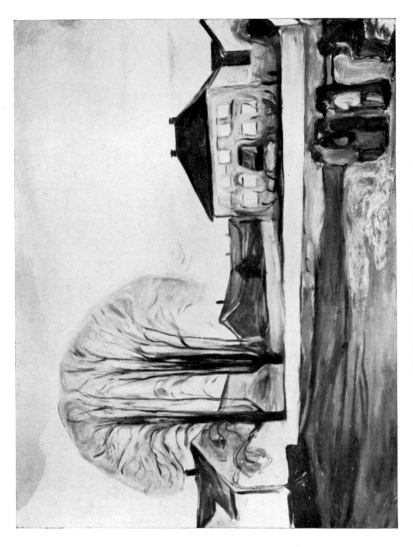

6. EDVARD MUNCH (1863–1944)
House under the trees. 1905
Folkwang Museum, Essen

7. OSKAR KOKOSCHKA
Santa Maria della Salute. 1928
Mademoiselle Lindauer Collection, Paris

8. ANDRÉ DERAIN (1880–1954)
Portrait of Madame Renou. 1930
Photo: Alex Reid & Lefèvre, Ltd.

9. GEORGES ROUAULT (1871–1958)
Head of a clown. 1930

10. CHAIM SOUTINE (b. 1894)
The Maid of Honour
Paul Guillaume Collection

11. ALBERTO GIACOMETTI (*b.* 1901)
Sketch 1957
Collection Kunsthaus, Zürich

12. OTTO DIX (*b.* 1891)
Blond Girl. 1931
Photo: Hugo Erfurth, Dresden

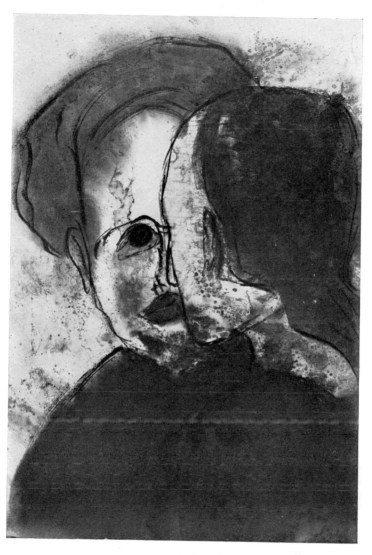

13. EMIL NOLDE (1867–1956)
Water-colour. 1931

14. CONSTANT PERMEKE (1886–1952)
The Harvesters. 1929

15. WILLIAM ROBERTS (*b.* 1895)
Dressmakers. 1932

16. GUSTAV DE SMET (1877–1943)
The Meeting. 1931
Photo: Editions Sélection, Antwerp

17. BEN SHAHN (*b*. 1898)
Father and child. 1946
James Thrall Soby Collection

18. GRAHAM SUTHERLAND (*b.* 1903)
Gorse on the sea-wall. 1939

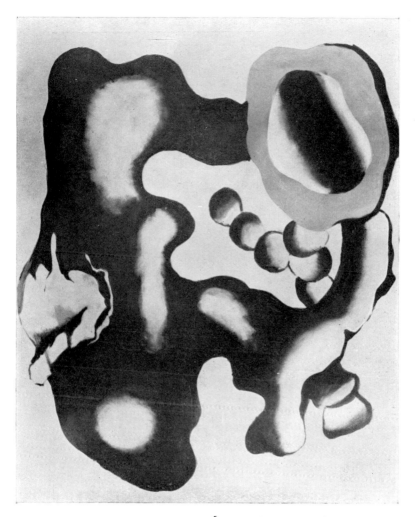

19. FERNAND LÉGER (1881–1955)
Pear-tree root. Gouache. 1932

20. MAX BECKMANN (1884–1950)
Nude. 1929
Rudolf Freiherr von Simolin Collection

21. HENRY MOORE (b. 1898)
Reclining figure. Elm wood. 1946
Cranbrook Academy of Art, Bloomfield Hills, U.S.A.

22. PAUL BERCOT (b. 1898)
Birth of the siren. 1943
Galerie Louis Carré, Paris

23. ANDRÉ FOUGERON (*b.* 1913)
Fish. 1946
Galerie Billiet-Caputo, Paris

24. JOHN MARIN (1870–1953)
Water-colour. Lower Manhattan. 1922.
Museum of Modern Art, New York

25. JEAN LE MOAL (*b.* 1909)
The Quay
Galerie René Drouin, Paris

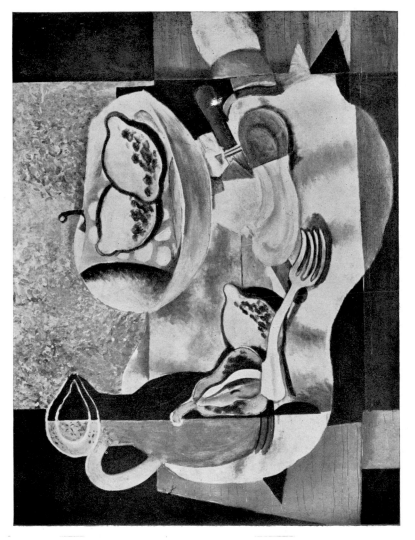

26. GEORGES BRAQUE (*b.* 1882)
Still-life. 1926
Paul Rosenberg Collection

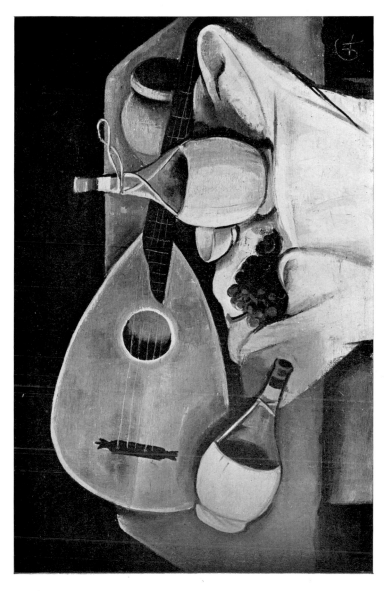

27. CARL HOFER (1878–1955)
Still-life. 1930
College Art Association, New York

28. GINO SEVERINI (b. 1883)
Les ruines antiques. Gouache. 1929

29. GEORGES BRAQUE
Still-life. 1931

30. KARL SCHMIDT-ROTTLUFF (*b.* 1884)
At the dressmaker's. 1928

31. ÉDOUARD PIGNON (*b.* 1905)
Pleureuse. 1946
Galerie de France, Paris

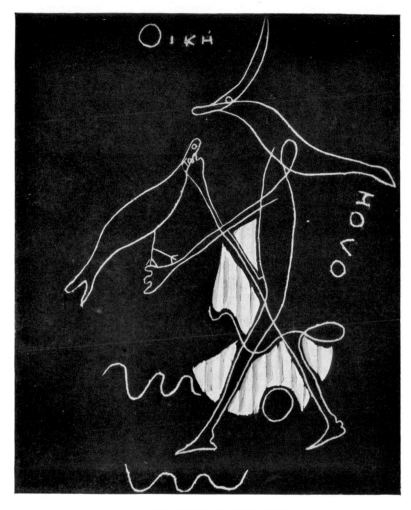

32. GEORGES BRAQUE
Greek Subject. 1933

33. ERNST LUDWIG KIRCHNER (1880–1938)
Dancing girl. 1931

34. JEAN DUBUFFET (*b.* 1902)
Figure with umbrella. 1945
Galerie René Drouin, Paris

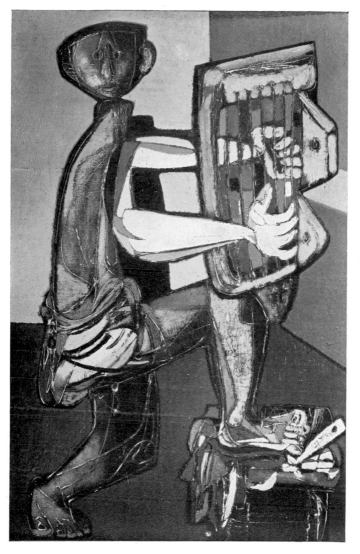

35. JANKEL ADLER (1896–1949)
David. 1945

36. WILLY BAUMEISTER (1889–1955)
Mural painting: tennis. 1933

37. GRAHAM SUTHERLAND (*b.* 1903)
Thorns. Watercolour. 1945
The British Council, London

38. RUFINO TAMAYO (*b.* 1899)
Animals. 1941
Museum of Modern Art, New York

39. FRANZ MARC (1880–1916)
Forms in Conflict. 1914
Bayerische Staatsgemäldesammlungen, Munich

40. HENRI LAURENS (*b.* 1885)
Océanide. Plaster. 1932
By permission of Cahiers d'Art

41. PABLO PICASSO (*b.* 1881)
Two Women. 1920
Paul Rosenberg Collection

42. HENRY MOORE
Madonna and child. 1944
Church of S. Matthew, Northampton

43. HENRY MOORE
King and Queen. 1952–3
W. J. Keswick Collection, Glenkiln

44. REG BUTLER (*b.* 1913)
The Manipulator. 1954

45. OSSIP ZADKIN (*b.* 1890)
The sculptor. Wood. 1933

46. PABLO PICASSO
Woman with fan. 1908
The Hermitage, Leningrad

47. PABLO PICASSO
Portrait of Vollard 1909–10
Pushkin Museum, Moscow

48. PABLO PICASSO
Still-life. 1913
Photo: Marc Vaux

49. PABLO PICASSO
The Woman with the golden breasts. 1913
Ingeborg Eichmann Collection

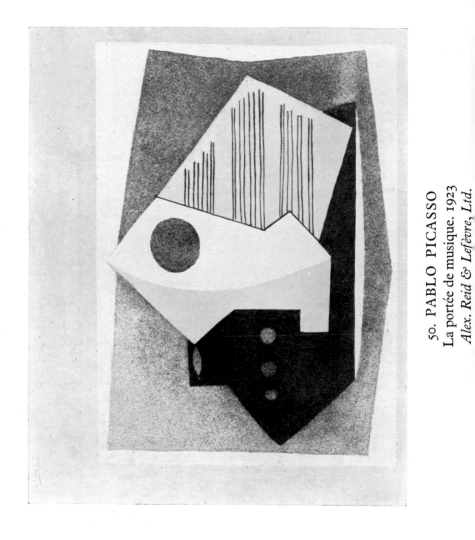

50. PABLO PICASSO
La portée de musique. 1923
Alex. Reid & Lefèvre, Ltd.

51. LOUIS MARCOUSSIS (1883–1941)
Figures at a table. 1930
Mayor Gallery, London

52. MARCEL DUCHAMP (*b.* 1887)
The king and queen crossed rapidly by nudes. 1912

53. MARIA ELENA VIEIRA DA SILVA (b. 1908)
Harbour—grey weather. 1952
Photo: Redfern Gallery, London

54. GONZALEZ (1876–1942)
Composition. 1931
Photo: Cahiers d'Art

55. KURT SCHWITTERS (1887–1947)
Grey-rose picture. 1932
Museum für Kunst und Landesgeschichte, Hanover

56. BEN NICHOLSON
Painted relief. 1944–5
Margaret Gardiner Collection

57. PIET MONDRIAN (1872–1944)
Composition B with red. 1935
Miss Helen Sutherland Collection

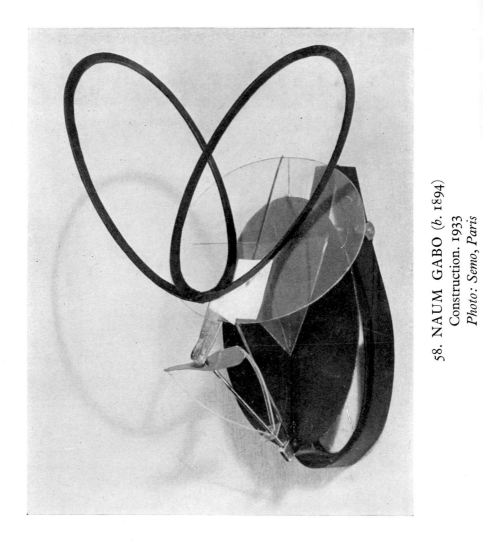

58. NAUM GABO (b. 1894)
Construction. 1933
Photo: Semo, Paris

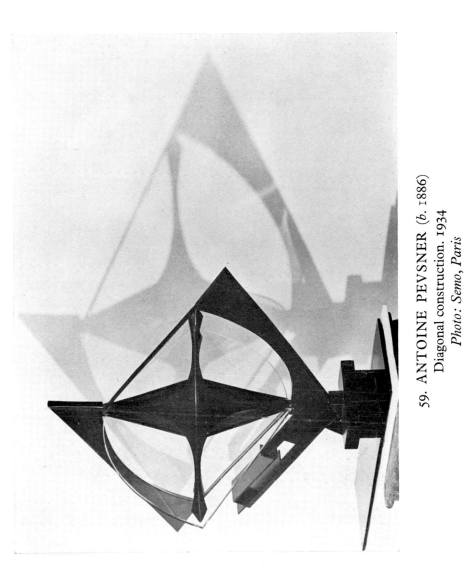

59. ANTOINE PEVSNER (*b.* 1886)
Diagonal construction. 1934
Photo: Semo, Paris

60. NAUM GABO
Construction in space: spiral theme. 1941
Museum of Modern Art, New York

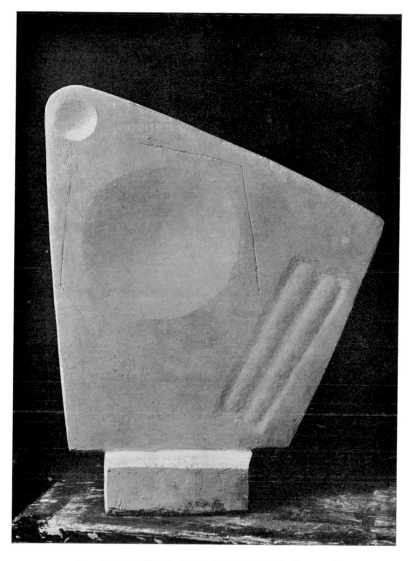

61. ALBERTO GIACOMETTI (*b.* 1901)
Personnage 1935
M. D. Whyte Collection

62. JACQUES LIPCHITZ (b. 1891)
Woman and guitar. Granite. 1928

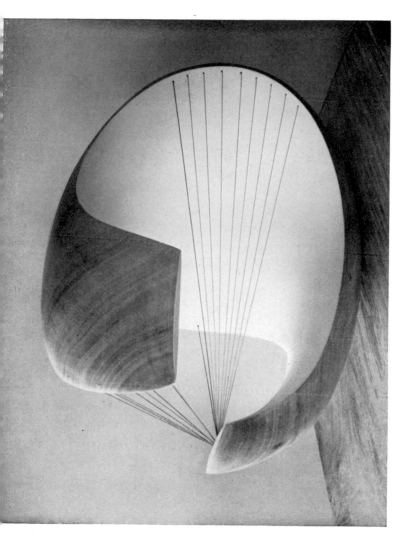

63. **BARBARA HEPWORTH** (*b.* 1903)
Sculpture: wood with colour. 1944
Ashley Havinden Collection

64. BARBARA HEPWORTH
Figure: Spanish mahogany. 1952

65. KARL HARTUNG (*b.* 1908)
Bronze 1941

66. ROBERT ADAMS (*b.* 1917)
Divided Pillar, 1952

67. JOHN WARREN DAVIS (*b.* 1919)
Dancer (*ciment fondu*). 1958

68. JUAN GRIS (1887–1927)
Harlequin with guitar. 1915
Marlborough Fine Art Ltd. London

69. ALBERT GLEIZES (*b.* 1881)
Composition. 1932

70. ROBERT DELAUNAY (1885–1941)
Legend. Mural painting. 1932

71. FRANK KUPKA (*b.* 1871)
The First Step. 1909
Museum of Modern Art, New York

72. I. RICE PEREIRA (*b.* 1905)
White lines. 1942
Museum of Modern Art, New York
(*Gift of Edgar Kaufmann, Jr.*)

73. L. MOHOLY-NAGY (1895–1946)
Construction. 1921–2

74. CASIMIR MALEVITCH (1878–1935)
Woman with Water Pails: Dynamic Arrangement 1912
Museum of Modern Art, New York

75. JEAN HÉLION (*b.* 1904)
Painting. 1935–6

76. SOPHIE TAUBER-ARP (1889–1943)
Six rooms. 1932

77. WASSILY KANDINSKY (1866–1944)
At Rest. 1928
Formerly in the Nationalgalerie, Berlin

78. LIONEL FEININGER (b. 1871)
The steamship 'Odin'. 1927
Photo: Lucia Moholy

79. WASSILY KANDINSKY
For and against. 1929
The Solomon R. Guggenheim Museum, New York

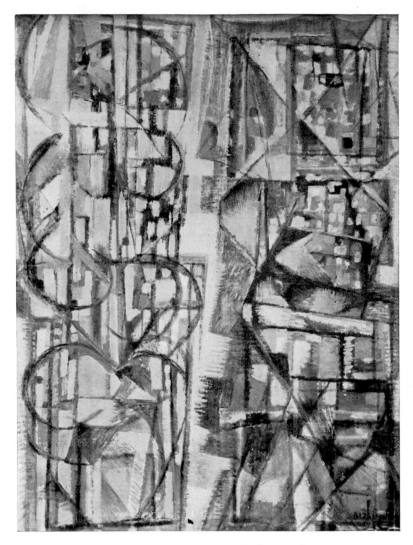

80. JEAN BAZAINE (*b.* 1904)
Promeneuse et nu au balcon. 1945
Galerie Louis Carrié, Paris

81. JEAN XCÉRON (*b.* 1890)
Composition: figures. 1932
By permission of Cahiers d'Art

82. FERNAND LÉGER
Composition. 1927

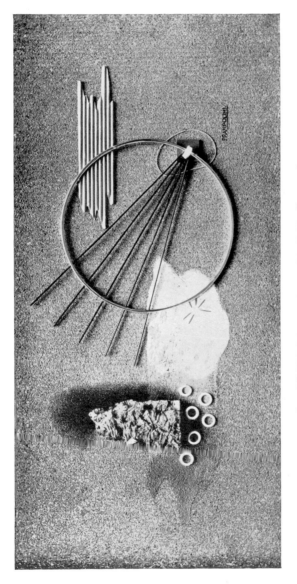

83. ENRICO PRAMPOLINI (*b.* 1894)
Abstract dimensions. 1933
Photo: C. Barucchello, Milan

84. CONSTANTIN BRANCUSI (1876–1957)
Socrates. Wood
Museum of Modern Art, New York

85. HENRY MOORE
String figure. *Lignum vitae* wood and string 1938
G. Burt Collection

86. FERNAND LÉGER (*b* 1881)
Composition. 1928
MacCormick Collection, Chicago

87. CHARLES LAPIQUE (*b.* 1898)
Canal in Champagne. 1943
Galerie Louis Carré, Paris

88. HANS ERNI (*b.* 1909)
Composition. 1935

89. CHARLES SMITH (*b.* 1893)
Horizontal arrangement. 1943
The Willard Gallery, New York

90. JEAN LURÇAT (b. 1894)
New York. 1930
Alex Reid & Lefèvre, Ltd

91. HANS ELTZBACHER (*b.* 1893)
Composition. 1932

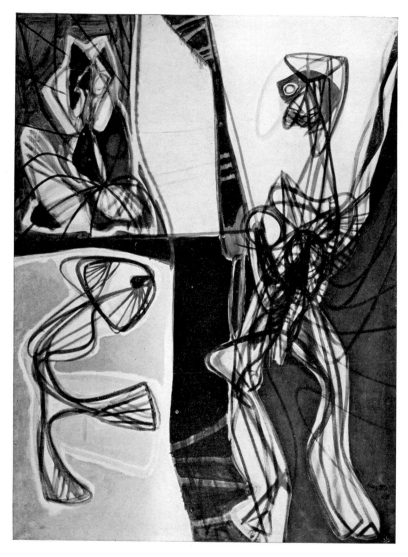

92. S. WILLIAM HAYTER (*b*. 1910)
Seated witness. 1945

93. ROY DE MAISTRE (*b.* 1898)
Seated figure. 1935
John Macmurray Collection

94. STUART DAVIS (*b.* 1894)
Salt shakers. 1931
Mrs. Edith Halpert Collection

95. ROBERT MOTHERWELL (*b.* 1915)
Figure. Collage: paper and egg-tempera 1945
Mr. and Mrs. George Wittenborn Collection

96. JACQUES VILLON (*b.* 1875)
Haute école au cirque, 1950

97. JOHN TUNNARD (*b.* 1900)
Journey (Gouache). 1955
Private Collection, London

98. MARC CHAGALL (*b.* 1887)
Lilac above the river. 1931
Josef von Sternberg Collection, Hollywood

99. HEINRICH CAMPENDONK (*b.* 1889)
The Red Shepherd

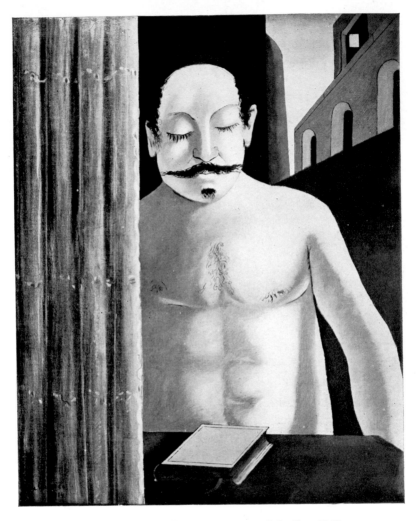

100. GIORGIO DE CHIRICO (*b.* 1888)
The Child's brain. 1914
André Breton Collection

101. GIORGIO DE CHIRICO
The Oracle. 1914
James Thrall Soby Collection

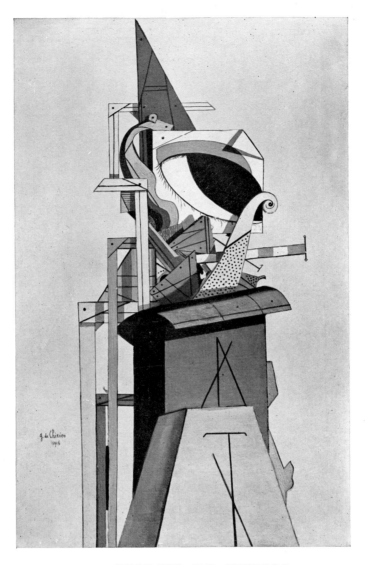

102. GIORGIO DE CHIRICO
The Jewish Angel. 1917
Roland Penrose Collection

103. RENÉ MAGRITTE (*b.* 1898)
The red model. 1935
Claude Spaak Collection

104. ANDRÉ MASSON (*b.* 1896)
Battle of the fishes. 1928

105. RENÉ MAGRITTE
The Forerunner. 1936
E. L. T. Mesens Collection

106. RENÉ MAGRITTE
La gravitation universelle. 1943
P. G. van Hecke-Norine Collection

107. PAUL DELVAUX (*b.* 1898)
The prisoner. 1942
M. van Hecke Collection

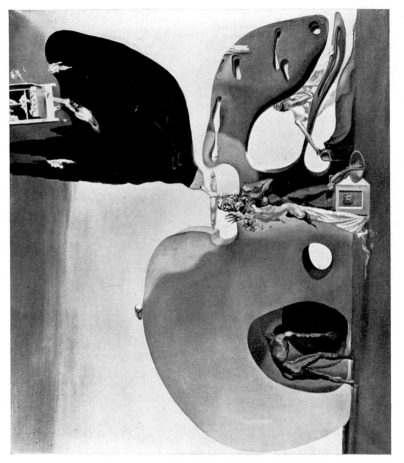

108. SALVADOR DALI (*b.* 1904)
Composition. 1933
Photo: Man Ray

109. SALVADOR DALI

Suburbs of the paranoiac-critical town (detail). 1935

Edward James Collection

110. PAUL NASH (1889–1946)
Salome. 1931
Private Collection, U.S.A.

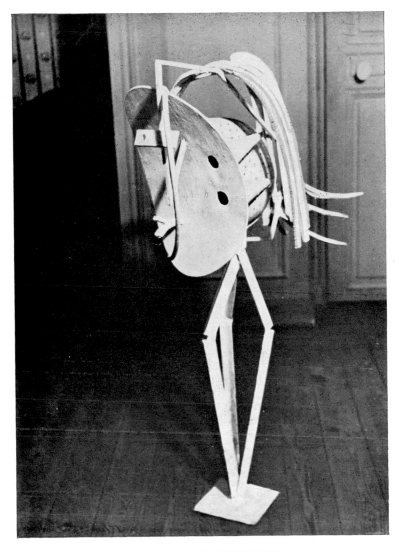

III. PABLO PICASSO
Metal sculpture. 1932
Photo: Brassai

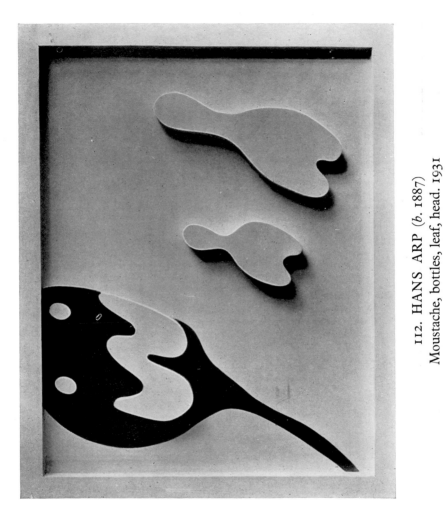

112. HANS ARP (b. 1887)

Moustache, bottles, leaf, head. 1931

113. HANS ARP
Mask. 1931

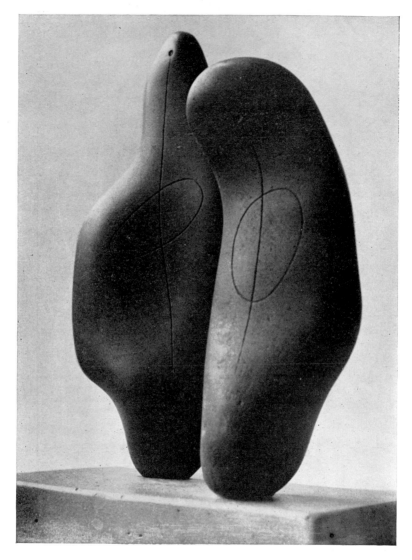

114. HENRY MOORE
Two forms. Ironstone. 1934
R. H. M. Ody Collection

115. HENRY MOORE
Bronze. Glenkiln Cross, 1955–6
W. J. Keswick Collection

116. JACQUES LIPCHITZ (*b.* 1891)
Rape of Europa II. Bronze. 1938

117. JACQUES LIPCHITZ
Spring. Bronze. 1942

118. ALEXANDER CALDER (*b.* 1898)
Octopus. 1944

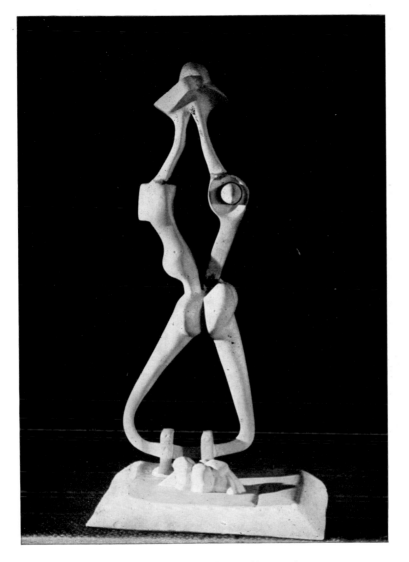

119. DAVID HARE (*b.* 1917)
Two. 1945

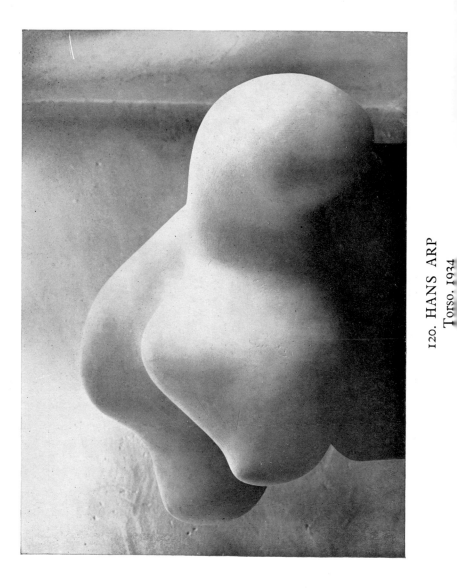

120. HANS ARP

Torso. 1934

121. HENRY MOORE
Reclining Figure. Bronze. 1953–4

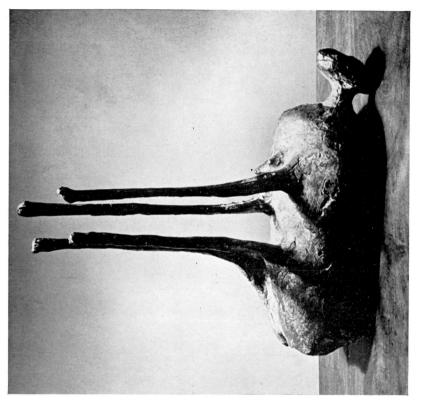

122. KENNETH ARMITAGE (b. 1916)
Roly-poly. 1955

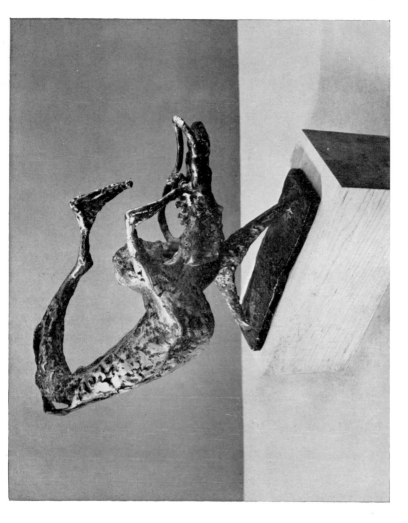

123. THEODORE J. ROSZAK (b. 1907)
Surge. Welded, hammered and brazed metal. 1946
Museum of Modern Art, New York

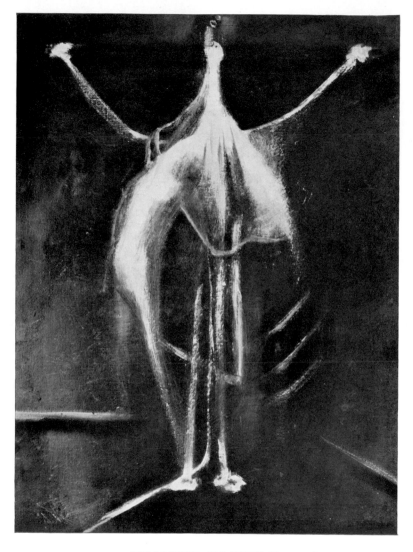

124. FRANCIS BACON (*b.* 1910)
Crucifixion. 1933
Photo: Mayor Gallery

125. JOHN HOSKINS (*b.* 1921)
Suncat. 1958

126. JOAN MIRÓ
Painting. 1927
Photo: Giraudon, Paris

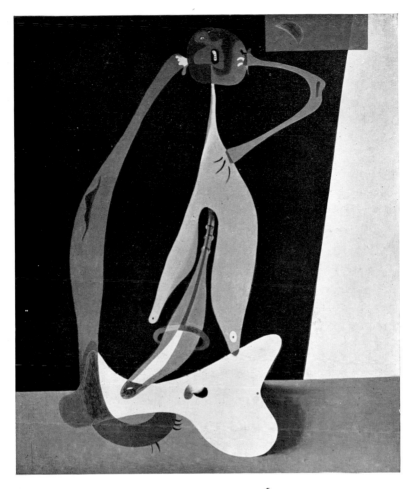

127. JOAN MIRÓ
Femme assise. 1932
James Johnson Sweeney Collection, New York

128. PABLO PICASSO
Abstraction. 1930
Alex. Reid & Lefèvre, Ltd.

129. CLYFFORD STILL
Painting 1951
Museum of Modern Art, New York

130. MAX ERNST (*b.* 1891)
Couple zoomorphe en gestation. 1933

131. MAX ERNST
A l'intérieur de la vue: l'oeuf. 1930
Photo: Mayor Gallery

132. PABLO PICASSO
Abstraction. 1929
Paul Rosenberg, Paris

133. ARTHUR DOVE (*b*. 1880)
Portrait of Frank Dusenberg. 1925

134. PABLO PICASSO
Large head with round eye. Plaster. 1932
Photo: Brassai

135. PABLO PICASSO
Woman reading. 1932
Samuel Marx Collection, Chicago

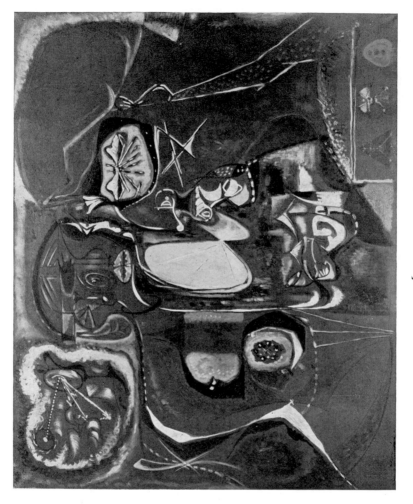

136. ANDRÉ MASSON (*b.* 1896)
da Vinci and Isabella d'Este. 1942

137. MATTA (Sebastian Antonio Matta Echaurren, *b.* 1912)
Les vertiges d'Eros. 1944
Museum of Modern Art, New York

138. EUGÈNE DE KERMADEC (b. 1899)
Woman with lamp. 1945
Galerie Louise Leiris

139. JACKSON POLLOCK (1912–1956)
Totem (lesson I). 1945

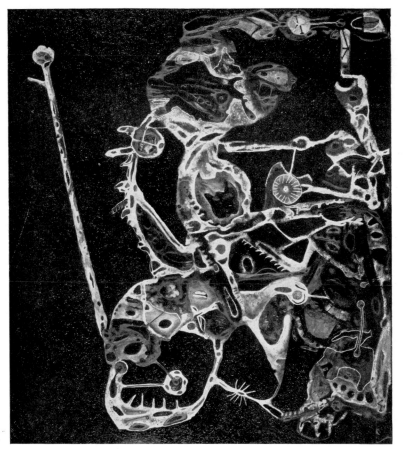

140. CHARLES SELIGER (b. 1926)
Don Quixote. 1944

141. ARSHILE GORKY (1904–1948)
Impatience. 1945
Mrs. Yves Tanguy Collection

142. MAX ERNST
Garden aeroplane-trap. 1934

143. PAUL NASH
Encounter in the afternoon. 1936
Edward James Collection

144. YVES TANGUY (1900–55)
The extinction of the species. 1936

145. JIMMY ERNST (*b.* 1920)
The Flying Dutchman. 1942
Museum of Modern Art, New York

146. ANDRÉ MASSON
Homage to John Donne. 1942

147. SALVADOR DALI
Drawing. 1936

148. PAUL KLEE (1879–1940)
Tight-rope dancer. 1923

149. PAUL KLEE
Gay breakfast table. 1928
Mrs. Stanley Resor Collection, New York

150. PAUL KLEE
Gay mountain landscape. 1929

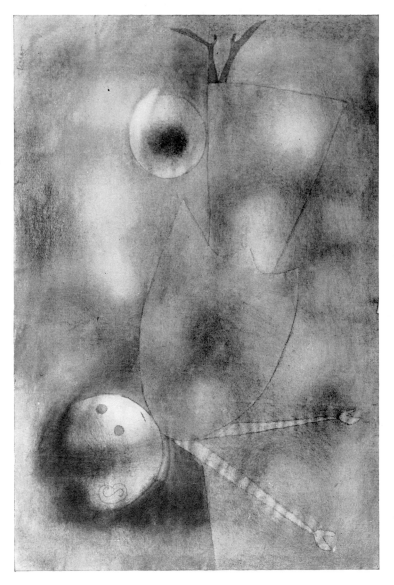

151. PAUL KLEE
Ball and doll. 1935

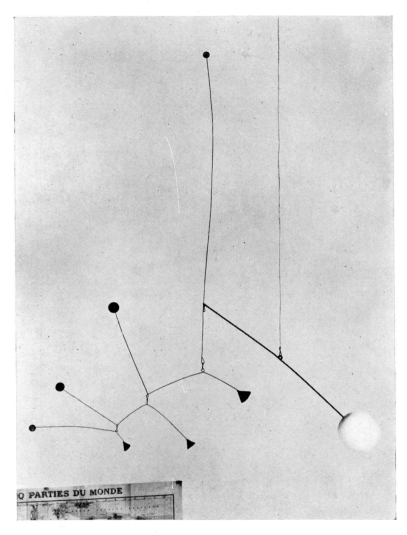

Q PARTIES DU MONDE

152. ALEXANDER CALDER (*b.* 1898)
Mobile. 1933

153. ALEXANDER CALDER
Constellation with red object, wood and steel rods. 1943
Museum of Modern Art, New York

154. SCOTTIE WILSON (b. 1890)
Drawing. *J. B. Brunius Collection*

155. MORRIS HIRSHFIELD (*b.* 1872)
Nude at the window. 1941
Martin Janis Collection, Hollywood

156. MORRIS GRAVES (b. 1910)
Little known bird of the inner eye. Gouache. 1941
Museum of Modern Art, New York

157. DARREL AUSTIN (*b.* 1907)
Catamount. 1940
Museum of Modern Art, New York

158. SIMON HANTAI (*b.* 1922)
Cut emerald eye. 1950
The Solomon R. Guggenheim Museum, New York

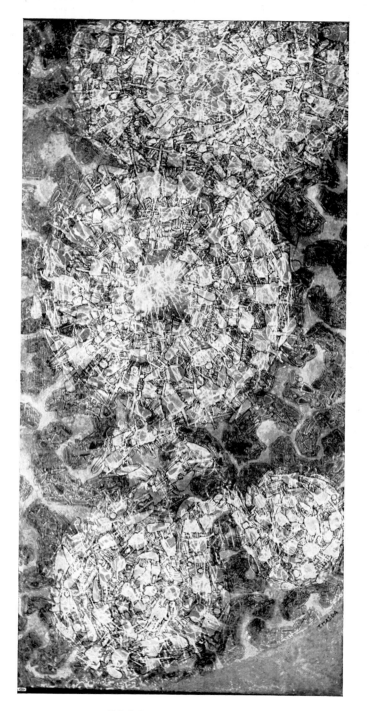

159. JOSAKU MAEDA (*b.* 1926)
Human landscape

160. MARK TOBEY (*b.* 1890)
Electric Night. 1950
Seattle Art Museum

161. MARK TOBEY
Space Ritual. 1958
Ortum Photos, Rome

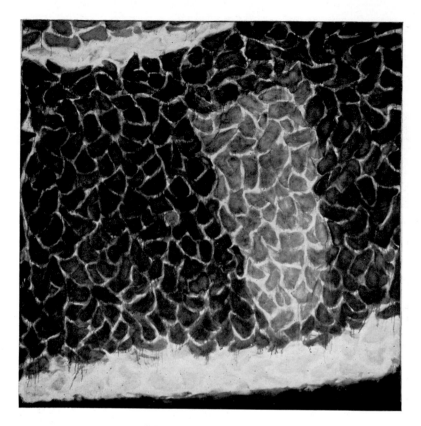

162. SAM FRANCIS (*b.* 1923)
Painting. 1953
Ortum Photos, Rome

163. RUTH FRANCKEN (*b.* 1924)
Unfolding. 1959
Photo: Robert David

164. HENRI MICHAUX (*b.* 1899)
Mescalin drawing. 1958
Photo: Henri Glaeser

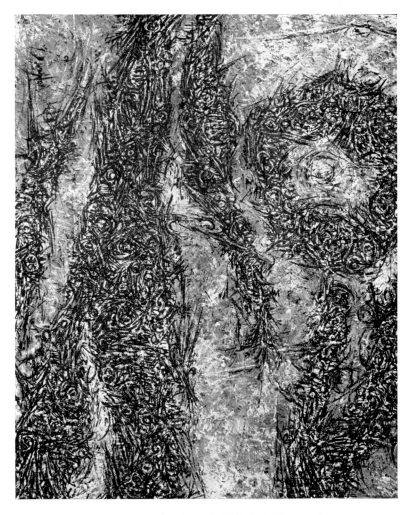

165. IAROSLAV SERPAN (*b.* 1922)
Painting. 1957
Collection David Thompson, Pittsburg

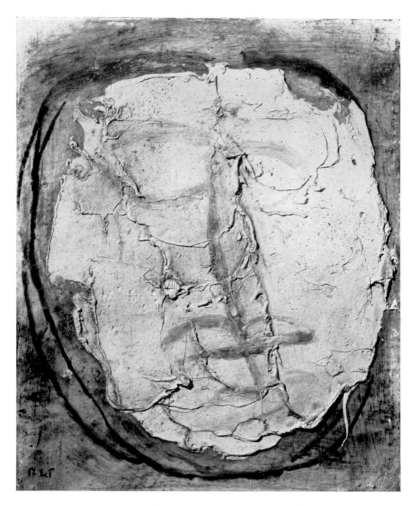

166. JEAN FAUTRIER (*b.* 1898)
Otage No. 12. 1945
Photo: Hanover Gallery

167. RENÉ GUIETTE (*b*. 1893)
Vertu 1958

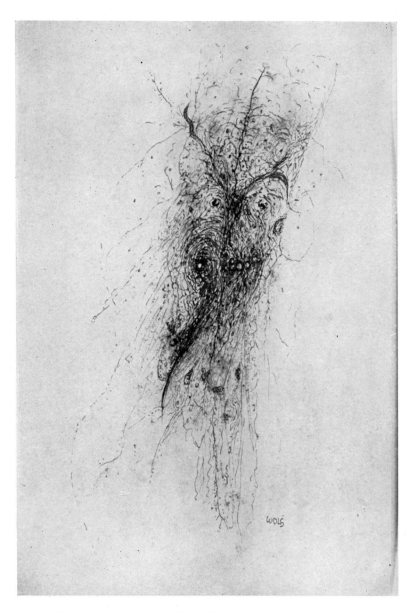

168. WOLS (Otto Alfred Schülze Battman, 1913–51)
Le Sorcier, 1942
Photo: Hanover Gallery

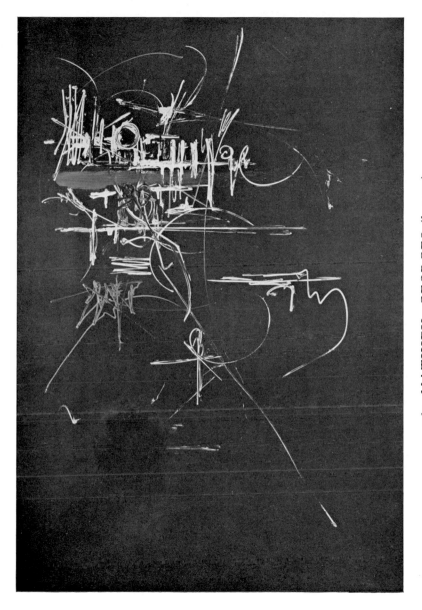

169. MATHIEU, GEORGES (b. 1921)
Painting. 1952
Solomon R. Guggenheim Museum, New York

170. JEAN PAUL RIOPELLE (*b.* 1924)
Repaire, 1957
Collection Lady Rothschild

171. CLAUDE GEORGES (*b.* 1929)
Painting. 1958
Photo: René Drouin, Paris

172. PIERRE SOULAGES (*b*. 1919)
Painting. 1953
Solomon R. Guggenheim Museum, New York

173. ADOLF GOTTLIEB (*b.* 1903)
Blast II. 1957
Joseph E. Seagram & Sons, New York

174. FRANZ KLINE (*b.* 1910)
Painting. 1952
Solomon R. Guggenheim Museum, New York

175. NICOLAS DE STAËL
Composition, 1953
Photo: Hanover Gallery

176. WILLEM DE KOONING (*b.* 1904)
Composition. 1955
Solomon R. Guggenheim Museum, New York

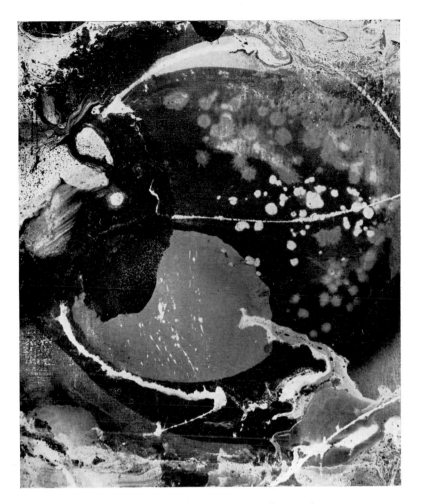

177. PAUL JENKINS (*b.* 1923)
Uranus. 1956
Photo: Paul Facchetti

178. JACKSON POLLOCK (1912–56)
The Deep. 1953
Lee Krasner Pollock Collection, Springs, Long Island, N.Y.

179. ALBERTO BURRI (*b.* 1915)
Grande Legno. 1958

180. SERGE POLIAKOFF (*b.* 1906)
Composition. 1957
Collection Dr. Jesi, Milan

181. VICTOR PASMORE (*b.* 1908)
Square motif in red. 1950

182. GIUSEPPE SANTOMASO (*b.* 1907)
Painting. 1952

183. ANTONIO TAPIES (*b.* 1923)
Peinture sable. 1957

184. EMILIO VEDOVA (*b.* 1919)
Image of Time, 1957
Collection Wise, U.S.A.

185. BRAM VAN VELDE (*b.* 1895)
Painting. 1948
Galerie Maeght, Paris

186. RENÉ ACHT (*b.* 1920)
Touch I. 1959
Ortum Photos, Rome

187. ALFRED MANESSIER (*b.* 1911)
Variation of Games in the Snow. 1951
Solomon R. Guggenheim Museum, New York

188. KAREL APPEL (*b.* 1921)
Portrait of the sculptor, César. 1956
Photo: Hanover Gallery

189. GERMAINE RICHIER (1904–1959)
Figure. 1952
Lead and Coloured glass
Photo: Robert Descharnes

190. MARINO MARINI (*b.* 1901)
Figures and Rider. 1931
Low relief in bronze
Alan Roger Collection, London

191. LYNN CHADWICK (*b.* 1914)
Dance. 1955
Iron and composition
Photo: David Farrell

192. ETIENNE MARTIN (*b.* 1913)
La Nuit. 1957
Ortum Photos, Rome